adversity

adversity

BUT THERE'S HOPE AHEAD

Richard T. Case

elevate
faith

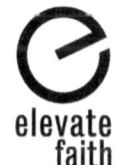

©2014 by Richard T. Case

All rights reserved. No portion of this book may be reproduced, stored in a retrieval system, or transmitted in any form or by any means—electronic, mechanical, photocopy, recording, scanning, or other—except for brief quotations in critical reviews or articles, without the prior written permission of the publisher.

Originally published by Milestone Publishing House, Dallas/Fort Worth, Texas.

Currently published by Elevate Faith. A division of Elevate Publishing, Boise, Idaho.

Cover & Interior Design by Roy Roper, wideyedesign.net

All Scripture Quotations marked MSG are from
The Message © 1993, 1994, 1995, 1996, 2000, 2001, 2002 by Eugene H. Peterson.

All Scripture Quotations marked NIV are from THE HOLY BIBLE, NEW INTERNATIONAL VERSION®, NIV® © 1973, 1978, 1984, 2010 by Biblica, Inc.™ Used by permission. All rights reserved worldwide.

All Scripture quotations marked ESV are from the english standard version.
© 2001 by Crossway Bibles, a division of Good News Publishers.

All Scripture quotations marked KJV are from The King James Bible. Public Domain.

All Scripture quotations marked ASV are from NEW AMERICAN STANDARD BIBLE®.
© The Lockman Foundation 1960, 1962, 1963, 1968, 1971, 1972, 1973, 1975, 1977. Used by permission.

ISBN: 978-1-943425-39-6
Ebook ISBN: 978-1-943425-38-9
Printed in the USA

contents

FOREWORD VII
INTRODUCTION 1

section 1
Understanding of Life Planned and Effect of the Fall 5

chapter 1   GOD'S ORIGINAL PLAN FOR MANKIND 6
chapter 2   A PROBLEM – THE FALL 13
chapter 3   THE FATHER HAS ANOTHER PLAN TO RESTORE THE ORIGINAL PLAN: CHRIST, OUR REDEEMER, OUR RESTORER 20
               SUMMARY OF SECTION 1 26

section 2
Understanding the Causes of Adversity and
God's Desire for our Response to this Adversity 31

chapter 4   GENERAL ADVERSITY 34
chapter 5   TEST OF FAITH 42
chapter 6   PRUNING 47
chapter 7   SELF-CENTEREDNESS 55
chapter 8   DISCIPLINE 61
chapter 9   JUDGMENT 65
chapter 10   ATTACK OF SATAN: CIRCUMSTANCES AGAINST US 69
chapter 11   ATTACK OF SATAN: PERSECUTION 79
chapter 12   HOW DO I KNOW WHICH ADVERSITY I AM FACING? 88

conclusions 93

foreword

There is a great deal of brokenness all over the world today and everyone has experienced some level of adversity and trial in their lives. Some people ask "why do bad things happen to good people" and others just accept it as a part of life. Most conclude it is luck or chance that some people are "more lucky" than others. This is particularly true when they see "bad people prospering" and thus conclude that there is really no way to truly understand or change their circumstances. This is particularly true when the belief is that God is in control so what is happening must be His will. There is also much confusion about pre-destiny and that God has chosen in advance what will happen in our lives and who will receive blessing and who will have difficulty.

In this book on Adversity, Rich Case examines Scripture in an in depth way to understand God's perspective and what He has to say about how and why these things happen. Most Christians today do not understand and few pastors are able to help them see why or teach on it. The result is we conclude that God is really not that good or we are not one of the lucky ones. Neither is true and are lies and deception of satan to keep us in bondage rather than living lives of peace, joy and abundance that would attract others and advance the kingdom of God.

Rich and Linda Case have been serving the Lord for over 30 years through their ministry All For Jesus Living Waters. They lead retreats focused on intensive study of the Word of God and weekly discipling calls studying topics such as Abiding, Unity, Living in the Kingdom, Possessing the Promised Land and the Remnant. They truly delight in sharing the Truths that the Lord has revealed through His Word and have been a blessing to many, helping them to learn to abide and hear from God.

Rich has been gifted by the Lord with wisdom and understanding of His Word and the ability to communicate in a way that is clear and concise and rooted in scripture. Most who read Adversity will have their fundamental beliefs and paradigms challenged and will be confronted with Truth that they will have to decide to accept or not. God desires that His people live in such a way that others will see His blessing and goodness in their lives and thus be drawn to it. As His witnesses to the world we are blessed to be a blessing – to make Him known and bear

INTRODUCTION

witness to the Truth that Jesus has come that we may have life and have it abundantly. Not in a material sense (although abundant life includes that) but a peace and joy that is His plan for the restored Kingdom. "And this eternal life that they may know you the only true God and Jesus Christ whom you have sent."

So, take the time to digest the material in this book, being diligent to go through the scriptures and journal your thoughts about what they are saying to you. In this way, we "abide in His Word and are His disciples indeed and we shall know the Truth and the Truth shall set us free" from the lies of satan about the cause and nature of adversity.

Press on !
David Dunkel, *CEO of K-Force*

introduction

Almost all the people attending our Living Waters Spiritual Retreats have much confusion about God's goodness and their personal experience of adversity (things not going well in their life). They view life through their difficult experiences, and thus, their real (true in their soul) perspective is that God is really not *that* good. This is based on faulty understanding of God and our life here in this world. They have been taught:

1. God is in control of everything

2. Thus, God is in control of my life.

3. Thus, everything that happens to me is God's will. Since He is in control, whatever happens to me must be His will.

4. Lots of very difficult things have happened to me, are happening

adversity

to me, and it looks like it's not getting better; or when things do get better, another difficult thing happens right behind it. This is certainly not the wonderful life that I had planned out or thought was going to happen, especially being a believer and a child of God.

5. Thus, it appears that others have God's favor and blessing that is spoken of in Scripture, but not me.

6. The only conclusion that can be drawn (not said in the intellect or to others, since that is not what Christians are supposed to say) is that God just is not that good – at least not to me. Why does all this bad stuff happen in the world, and especially to me, if He is in control? No matter how much I try to say, "This must be God's will for my own good, and I am supposed to just live with it" – we call this Christian fatalism – my heart just cannot accept it (and rightly so);

7. So, underneath it all, there is a deep disappointment with God, a degree of anger and resignation. Then this results in me not having an intimate relationship with God through abiding in the Word, through prayer, and in the Spirit. Why bother? It does not seem to matter. Further, the best thing I can do is work really hard with my best thinking to try to overcome my adversities and

INTRODUCTION

hope that God does some things to help me. Though, if things do seem to get better, I do not expect this to last. I will pray, put on the smiling Christian face and say things are fine, but I do not really expect answers to prayers and will likely continue to have difficulty.

This has been a nifty trick of the enemy. The very conclusions we reach and the acceptance of the adversity as normal actually serves to perpetuate our adversity. We do know there is an enemy, but since God is in control and has gained victory over principalities and powers at the cross, does He not have the ability to keep him away from my life? Hey, why is all this happening to me; and is there any hope at all, or are we just to accept this very difficult life as normal? Should we accept that we are sinners and going to fail, that bad things happen, and that God uses it all to teach us things? But underneath it all, we still do not see God as very good and it seems rather cruel for Him to not be taking better care of His children. If it were me, I would.

This book will take you through the Word to help you see the truth that God is absolutely good! He has wonderful plans for us. We will experience adversity. Some is normal, as the bible tells us that in this world we will have trouble. Some is from God, and much is not, but the good news is that there are remedies for all of them. Please take the time to process the Word in each chapter so that you can personally receive the truths laid out. My prayer is that your heart is opened to receive what He desires to reveal to you and that it will free you for the grand plans He has in store for your life.

section 1
UNDERSTANDING OF LIFE PLANNED AND EFFECT OF THE FALL

Adversity did not just come upon mankind as part of God's original plan, rather it came upon us as a result of the Fall of Adam and Eve, who exercised their self will, disobeyed God's instruction to not eat of the tree of the Knowledge of Good and Evil, and died as God had warned (meaning the Holy Spirit departed from their nature). As a result, Satan gained authority and power over this earth; and this power is pure destruction – designed to kill, steal and destroy. Adversity came about because of man's selfishness and the opposing power of Satan that is now operating where things are difficult, painful, frustrating, hard, annoying, oppressive, confusing, etc. Adversity is normal and ever present. In order to recognize the various forms of adversity and to know how to deal with it, we first must understand God's original plan for mankind, the effect of the Fall upon us and our lives, and God's remedy of redemption.

chapter 1
GOD'S ORIGINAL PLAN FOR MANKIND

God's original plan for mankind is recorded in Genesis 1 and 2, which was written before the fall. He set forth the exceptional life that Adam and Eve enjoyed before the fall, which was His original plan. In chapters 2 and 3, it is revealed what life with Him looks like after the fall. This exceptional life included these seven exceptional gifts:

1. **Exceptional Authority:**
   Victory & Power to Loose & Bind

   Authority is defined in the Scriptures as Dominion and Power manifested in many different ways:

   - Splendor, majesty, beauty, vigor, glory

   - In-charge, control, have jurisdiction, power to influence

- Cause to become: great; much; many; enlarged, exceedingly abundant

- Power (physical & spiritual) of doing the supernatural.

- Right to govern, rule, command - possessing authority

- Mighty work, strength, miracle

- Performing miracles

- Excellence

Gen 1:1–3: First, we must understand the very nature of God's creation: He "spoke" it into existence from nothing (ex-nihilo). God is Spirit – invisible, omniscient, omnipresent, omnipotent. All authority emanates from Him, as He is and has the ultimate authority, which is the ability to create material from the Spiritual. His creation is from His spoken Word (John 1: 1 – 3). The Spiritual trumps the material and is superior to the material; thus, the material is subordinate to the Spiritual and under its authority. This is key for us to understand, as it explains why nothing is too difficult for Him; and why His power can change our circumstances, especially the adversity against us.

Gen 1:26–27: God created man in "Our" image. Who is "Our"? It is the Trinity – the Father, Son and Holy Spirit are the triune God. One God, yet each distinct, and all the nature and characteristics of God are resident in all three. This includes authority. God originally gave this authority (dominion) over the mankind to rule the earth and be co-creators with Him in perfect communion with Him as created beings – with body (material), soul (seat of our personality, intellect, emotion, and will) and Spirit (His Spirit in us as ruler and leader of our lives). We were to live out this authority on earth as we walked with Him and subdued the earth under the authority given us.

2. Exceptional Provision:

Gen 1:28–30: God provided all that was needed to live and enjoy the fullness of His creation – all the plants, animals, and materials (organic and inorganic) were all created so that we lacked nothing. God's creation was all for our benefit of use, to build, and to make new things as we were led through being co-creator with Him – and all this was subordinate to the Spiritual. The Word "give" means that He grants us, gives over to us, and delivers up to us all this exceptional provision. We would never be short of anything needed and were to enjoy abundance, so we would not have to be concerned about living conditions or making things work in this material world.

3. Exceptional Work:

Gen 2: 15: God gave to man and woman the assignment of "Work" –

occupation and labor that served the purposes of God. They were to keep and care for this world through daily, meaningful occupation – which is simply defined as what we "do" every day to occupy our time in tasks for the benefit of progress and co-creating with God. Thus, this is not about earning income, but rather working at something we truly enjoy. So a housewife who thoroughly enjoys taking care of children and the duties of being a wife is in an exceptional "occupation." We must understand that this is a part of God's nature that was given to mankind before the fall – work is good and to be fulfilled by all of us. It brings much to us in the form of satisfaction, fulfillment, accomplishment, community with others, joy and fun.

4. Exceptional Marriage:

Gen 2:18–25: God said it is not good that man be alone, so he created "Wo-man" out of man, to be a helpmate, his counterpart in intimate relationship while living here on earth. He said the two are to leave their father and mother. It is interesting that Adam and Eve had no mother and father. So, of what was He speaking? He was saying that all who were to come thereafter were to leave their upbringing behind and forge a new way together as a couple – to come together as one – living in unity and agreement. They were to live this way only with each other, as together they walked in the Spirit in complete unity with God, with the authority and dominion given to them as co-creators over earth. As we live in unity in our exceptional marriage, it will be a place of blessing.

In **Psalm 133**, God states that it is good (most wonderful and favorable) and pleasant (delightful, lovely, fantastic) to dwell (live in) unity (united-ness, agreement, oneness). There He commands (orders, brings about with certainty) blessings – gifts of favor, prosperity, good things. So, through living in an exceptional marriage in unity, He promises His favor in life. Why would we not live there?

Note: Think about God's original plan for mankind: Since we are physical, and thus, need to sleep for rest and recuperation, then we are to get up to go to Work and enjoy our exceptional occupation during the day; then, after work we are to go home and enjoy our exceptional marriage and family life. Ecclesiastes 5:18–20; 9:9–10: God tells us there is nothing more important than enjoying our work and our marriage/family. It is to be the primary reason to rejoice and experience life to the full.

5. Exceptional Identity:

Gen 1:26; 1:31: Adam and Eve understood that they were made in the likeness of God and were the children of the most High God. They embraced their identity and lived fully in the bounty of the exceptional life provided by God. They did not reject it, diminish it, nor compromise on it – they lived like children of the King – because they were! They were God's and they knew it. This is reiterated in **Song of Solomon 6: 3: "I am my beloved's and My beloved is mine."** We are His loved ones, special and privileged to be His children.

6. Exceptional Health and Healing:

Gen: 1:26 – 2:25: There was no sickness or illness in the Garden. God's exceptional life included health and healing. They lived in perfect health and enjoyed the beauty of not being concerned about physical issues.

7. Exceptional Communion with Him:

Gen: 1:26 – 2:25: Since Adam and Eve had body, soul and Spirit, they had exceptional communion with God. They had regular communications, heard clearly what He had to say, could dialogue with Him at any time, and enjoyed their designed intimacy with Him all the time. They were His children, lived in the beauty of a special relationship with the Almighty God, the creator of the universe, and had the confidence of knowing they were living in the exceptional life provided for and given by God. This is expressed further in **John 10:3–5; 27–30**. He is our Shepherd and knows us intimately – and we hear Him (attend to, consider what is or has been said; to understand, perceive the sense of what is said; to hear something; to perceive by the ear what is announced in

adversity

one's presence), know Him (to see; to perceive with the eyes; to perceive by any of the senses; to perceive, notice, discern, discover) and follow Him (willingly go with Him where He leads us). He also describes this in **John 15:1–8**. We are intimately connected to Him as the Branch to the Vine, with the Vinedresser (The Father) directing our lives through making our decisions. We remain in Him, and as a result, we bear fruit, more fruit, and much fruit. We glorify Him, as we abide in Him through our intimate relationship. As Adam and Eve fully understood, "Apart from Him we can do nothing." Why? Because of exceptional communion. How special is that!

Summary: In **Gen 1:31** it states: "Then God saw everything (all these exceptional characteristics of life with Him) that He had made, and indeed it was very good. So the evening and the morning were the sixth day. The earth was perfect. It had no destructive forces, no sin, no pain, no sickness, and no adversity. All was good – exceptionally and abundantly good! This Hebrew word is a very strong definition of what "good" means - pleasant, agreeable (to the senses); *pleasant (to the higher nature), excellent, rich, valuable in estimation: glad, happy, prosperous.* These seven exceptional qualities of God's creation before the fall were amazingly, extraordinarily, supernaturally good. This was God's original plan – nothing but spectacular with no adversity - life abundant and life eternal. We must understand this as we look at the current state of the world with its common and normal adversity.

chapter 2
A PROBLEM – THE FALL

This wonderful life ended. In **Genesis 3:1–13**, we see what happened. Satan had already been booted out of heaven. As Lucifer (an angel of light), he was number two in heaven with all the wonder and beauty of heaven, but decided with his free will to not choose God. God's creation of his higher beings – angels and man – include free will. True love is based upon free will – the ability to choose God or not. In **Isaiah 14:12–21**, we read that Lucifer wanted to be like God made a move to take over. Not having the power of God (we must remember that Satan is not God – not all omniscient, omnipresent, omnipotent – but a created being with limitations), he did not win this challenge to God through this free will and was consequently cast out of heaven. In addition to all the angels in heaven (150,000,000 , Revelation 5:11 states there are 10,000 X 10,000

adversity

angels now in heaven which equals 100,000,000. These angels represent 2/3 of the total. (1/3 chose to go with Satan, Revelation 12:4), exercised their free wills and chose to also reject God and follow Satan. So, now Satan and his 50,000,000 demons had access to earth and to Adam and Eve, but he had no authority to bring his destruction. So what he had to do was appeal to Adam and Eve to exercise their free will and disobey God, so that Satan could receive the authority given to Adam and Eve (in Gen. 1:26 where this authority was given to mankind), and thereby, alter the nature of earth to be dominated by Satan's nature of destruction. Satan appealed to Eve, and thus, to Adam who was right there with her to choose to eat of the forbidden tree (the tree of the knowledge of good and evil in the middle of the garden). This tree was designated by God so that there was a real choice of exercising their free will, which included the free will to either choose God or not, as had Lucifer and the demonic angels. The warning was that if they ate of this tree, they would surely die. Lucifer appealed to them that God surely did not say, "you would die," and do you not want to be like God? As is true with our free will today, the real mistake that Adam and Eve made at this point was wondering about what God really did say, and exactly what it meant. Also, they did not go back to God with their open, perfect and exceptional communion and ask God again to speak on this. They just drew their own conclusions, based upon the temptation of what they heard from Satan.

As a result, they ate of the forbidden tree. At that moment they did die, as spoken by God. What actually died? Man and woman were created as body (real material), soul (the seat of intellect, personality, emotion, and will) and spirit (God's Holy Spirit). Animals are just body and soul, and driven by instincts (self-preservation). So, at the fall, the spirit of man and woman died. The Holy Spirit had to vacate. They became a very sophisticated, intellectually superior animal now, driven by instinct and self-centeredness. Their nature changed. It became a sin nature devoid of the Spirit of God and not holy. This impeded their ability to have direct relationship with God, because He is holy and requires perfection. Thus, the nature of the world changed. It went from the beauty, perfection and all the exceptional goodness of God of His original creation to the nature of Satan. John 10:10 –tells us that Satan seeks to kill, steal and destroy. It must be noted that the only remedy is to be "born again" – to have the Spirit re-enter our nature and give us the ability to receive Christ's life in us. But at the fall, everything on earth (both animate and inanimate) went to and is still operating in destruction, called entropy. This includes all things, like steel bridges that collapse in Minneapolis, the coliseum in Rome, etc. So everything left alone will go to destruction, and this destructive world is being led by those in power who are fallen, sinful people who operate purely selfishly. Thus, it should not surprise us that the world is literally going to "hell in a hand basket" and getting more and more wicked, full of the values of anti-God. When Adam and Eve exercised their free will and disobeyed God's will, they thwarted the original plan of exceptional life in an exceptional creation and handed over the authority and sinful nature of man and the world destruction to Satan. The world is now a place of great trouble, great adversity, and great difficulty. This has become normal and is getting even more so:

- **The enemy's world in which we live: John 10:10** shows us that this is the essence of the enemy. He aims to kill (put to death good things); steal (take away by theft, i.e. take away by stealth); and destroy (to put out of the way entirely, abolish, put an end to ruin, render useless). It is relentless and never ending. There is no breather. The world in which we live is the world of the enemy, so naturally, it is a place where things oppose us and where things are not intended to go well for us. This is so that we do not seek God and learn to abide and remain in Him, but to rather blame God for these awful things that happen to us.

- **Luke 4: 5–8:** Satan tempts Christ by offering the Kingdoms of the World to Him to take a shortcut for why He has come, which is to take back the authority without having to go to the cross. The intent is for Christ to just subordinate Himself to Satan. This was a real temptation, which meant that Satan actually had the ability to deliver the Kingdoms of the World (which was now his since it was given to him by Adam and Eve). The Greek word "Kingdom" here means power, kingship, dominion, rule, the right or authority to rule over a kingdom; and "Power" is another word for authority and dominion. If it was not real, Christ would have dismissed it knowing that it was not Satan's to give, so nothing real was being offered. Rather, Christ said, "Yes, you do have this authority now," but He still chooses not to take a shortcut but only worship and follow the Father. His will was to choose God. **Note a very profound truth: Adam and Eve exercised self-will and fell into sin. The only way to restore this nature of sin now within all mankind born into the world from Adam and Eve was for God Himself (Christ) to exercise His self-will and not succumb to these temptations at the beginning of His ministry on earth. He then needed to exercise His self-will in Gethsemane on His way to the cross at the end of His ministry, so that based upon His free will (and it was purely His choice, as read in John 10: 17–18). He marched to the cross where the sin was placed upon Him and satisfied the Father's requirement of perfection (propitiation/ sacrifice), thus, He obtained back the authority for man to once again be "born again" thru belief. This enabled us to have**

adversity

the Holy Spirit restored in our nature. Christ did acknowledge that Satan had the authority of worldly kingdoms operating on earth and that the nature of his kingdoms was destruction – to steal, kill and destroy.

- **1 John 5: 18–20:** John wrote 60 years after the resurrection that Satan still had control over this world. Though Christ has taken back the authority, His authority operates in His Kingdom which now is available to us to live in; but we also live in the natural world that is still under the authority of Satan, which is what we would call enemy territory. The Greek word here for wickedness means: full of labor, annoyances, hardships, pressed and harassed, toil, full of peril, pain and trouble, bad, evil, wicked, and bad. That pretty well describes our world. It should not surprise us that this characterizes everyday life. Though believers, we live in enemy territory and are subject to this normal wickedness. As believers we are called to live in both kingdoms – within the Kingdom of God which is righteousness, peace and joy in the Holy Spirit (Romans 14:17), while we also traverse through enemy territory in a world under the control of the enemy. This world is still characterized by destruction – kill, steal and destroy. We must fully understand that though Satan has been defeated by Christ, and all authority has now been given to Christ, this is spiritual

SECTION I

authority, which does trump temporal authority. However, this is only appropriated by believers who are walking in the Spirit in His Kingdom. We exist within these two kingdoms. The worldly Kingdom is still the nature of entropy with dark principalities and powers still operating. We are not exempt from this kingdom, and adversity will still occur in our everyday lives.

The fall happened, and man received a self-centered sin nature, with which all are born, and the world went from being perfect with exceptional living to one of difficulty, adversity, and wickedness as the norm. We cannot escape it and are all subject to it.

chapter 3
THE FATHER HAS ANOTHER PLAN TO RESTORE THE ORIGINAL PLAN: CHRIST, OUR REDEEMER, OUR RESTORER

Though the world has been lost to destruction under the control of the enemy, and our nature is now a sin nature dominated by self. The Father has provided another plan. He has given us a Redeemer that can bring us again back to the beautiful, restored life intended by God. Salvation and being born again is not just a ticket to heaven, but it is an invitation to a restoration of the original, exceptional life intended by God in the Garden of Eden. Christ has come to bring us this exceptional life now.

- **John 10:10:** The words spoken by Christ here are the same words used by the Father in Genesis 1:31 – this life that Christ has come to give us is the exceptional, super abundant good life intended in the Garden of Eden. His death and resurrection conquered death and Satan, and thus, we do not have to live under the control and influence of the destructive enemy; but rather, we can reverse the destruction and receive to the point of possessing, owning, this super abundant (exceedingly, supremely, extraordinary, more remarkable, more excellent) life. This life is full, genuine, real, active, vigorous, fullness of life of God. This is to be lived out in this destructive world, as we live in the Kingdom of God, in the Spirit, and in Christ. It is not just for heaven but for the now. Thus, while we will have adversity since we live in enemy territory, we have this exceptional, abundant life offered to us.

- **Luke 4:16–21; Isaiah 61:1-5:** Luke 4 describes the first public statement of Christ about His ministry. He goes to the synagogue in Nazareth, which He had been to many times since He lived there, and is handed the Scroll of Isaiah 61 to read. He reads it and states publicly (after sitting down to make an emphatic point) that Isaiah 61 has been fulfilled in Him, and He has come to bring this redemptive, beautiful life to us now and not just a ticket to heaven. This beautiful life includes healing up our wounds (to bind up, repair). We are all wounded and have patterns in our lives that are destructive and cause us

adversity

difficulty. Christ promises to heal us so that these wounds are fully restored to health, and thus, no longer cause us difficulty and lead us to our poor responses to things in life. Instead, He gives us liberty (free-flowing freedom) and frees us up from being captive. Again, all of us are captive to certain patterns and ways of how we look at and respond to life. We can be living in un-forgiveness, full of anger, always frustrated, respond in fear, worry and anxiety, etc., and no matter how much we try, we cannot seem to live in freedom; and thus, we remain in our captivity. Christ promises us that He will lead us to freedom and release us from our patterns of captivity so that our life is full of joy and wonder; Christ gives us comfort (bring compassion, console, hope) when we are downtrodden, burdened, grieving, and disappointed, because the situations in our lives just are not working well or not what we thought they would be. We have a tendency to go to resignation and accept that this life is troublesome, is never going to be great (perhaps once in a while but certainly not as the norm), and we just have to put up with it. Christ promises that He will give us comfort and show us how wonderful life can be, as we walk with Him. He also promises that He can make beauty (ornaments, value) from ashes. Throughout our life, we often can ruin or have ruined things that literally are ashes – of no value and no hope of amounting to anything. Christ has such amazing supernatural power that He can bring worthless, dead things back to life, back to value, and back to such beauty that it is exceptional – the original exceptional life of Genesis. He can deliver joy and praise from things that have not gone well and are heavy and weighing on us. Instead of going to worry, fear and anxiety, He causes us to experience true joy and praise to the extent that we are thrilled at the life He has brought and the hope of the promises ahead even if experiencing difficulty now. Further, He promises to build up and repair from our ruins (construct, rebuild, re-establish to original, make new again). How cool is that? What we have ruined through our sin and lousy choices can all be restored to God's original plan, and it matters not how much it is ruined. This is the Good News. He can redeem and restore anything! He can take what has been ruined by the enemy (killed, stolen and destroyed) or by us through not following Him, and He can make it beautiful, restored, rebuilt, and restored. This sums up the wonderful ministry of Christ today. It's not just a ticket to heaven, but it has come to give us the abundant, exceptional life now that He has uniquely planned for us. Remember, He is not a respecter of persons, with some being lucky and others

adversity

not, This is why He has come and offers exceptional life to all who are His children.

So, the people of the world now have a clear choice. We can continue to live as self-centered people in a fallen world that is self-destructing, or we can live as a child of God that is redeemed. Then the children of God have two choices to make: (1) live in His Kingdom through abiding in Him ("Apart from Him we can do nothing" – John 15:5), walking in the Spirit, and thus, experiencing the restoration of the exceptional life ("I have come to give you life and give it super abundantly" – John 10:10); or (2) live a carnal life in the flesh (remain self-centered) and again put to death the Spirit (still resident in us, but operating as if not there), be at enmity against God's will (live outside his Kingdom life), and not able to please Him (Romans 8: 5–8). As we will see in Section 2, by living in the Kingdom and abiding and walking in the Spirit, we cannot avoid all adversity. There are certain ones that are brought purposely by God to cause us to repent and turn away from our carnal living as a believer, so these adversities will be experienced, though they need not be. For the unbeliever there is a deepening sense of adversity that characterizes their life on a global and national level, as well as on a personal level. There is judgment against mankind on a global, national, local and personal level, because the truth stands, regardless of whether we seek it or understand it; and there really is no excuse, since there is built within us a sense that there is something greater than us. There are plenty of physical indicators available to all who can see that there is something greater than us. Romans 1:18 and 2:16 explain this in great detail. The wrath (judgment of God) is revealed against all ungodliness, for God has revealed Himself to all, and thus, none are without excuse. They are living futile lives and are foolishly thinking they are wise having exchanged the glory of the incorruptible God for the corruptible idols of man. Because of this, God gives them over to their sad, adversity-filled lives and their evil passions (like homosexuality, greed, adultery, strife, deceit, etc.) that only promote more adversity. Those who are self-seeking and do not seek nor follow the truth, but rather pursue unrighteousness which they have believed to be righteous, will experience indignation, wrath, tribulation and anguish. In other words, they receive major adversity as normal. If we step from our own time back in history and look at all of history visiting each era and observing, we would basically see awful, difficult things and great adversity all over the place. Regardless of our station in life, none of us would want to go back to another time if we really knew what it was like. We Americans have been blessed, because we were a nation under God and received blessings of prosperity, standard of living, freedom, avoidance of war on our soil (except civil war between ourselves), and the expectation and hope that things would always get better. Thus, our level of general adversity (see description in Chapter 4) has been relatively protected and contained, because we were a nation under God. Today, I believe that is not so, and we are suffering the consequences of Romans 1 and 2 as a nation. God is giving over our nation to its uncleanness and vile passions, withdrawing His protection over adversity and actually bringing about His promised indignation, wrath, tribulation and anguish. It is going to get worse, and those of us who are still living in the Kingdom of God are not exempt from this global and national scale of adversity, which characterizes most of history on earth. Our lives are going to become more difficult, frustrating and painful, not because our government and rulers cannot quite get it right regardless of political persuasion, but because we are dealing in Spiritual things and live outside of God's protection, it will typically be full of adversity. This should not surprise us, nor should we think that we are exempt.

SUMMARY OF **section 1**

- God originally planned an exceptional life for His creation – mankind:
  - Exceptional Authority

SECTION I

- Exceptional Provision
- Exceptional Work
- Exceptional Marriage
- Exceptional Identity
- Exceptional Health & Healing
- Exceptional Communion with God

Adam and Eve fully enjoyed this life in the Garden of Eden. It was theirs to enjoy, and it truly was exceptional. This life is a picture for us to see as His original plan; a plan though lost through the fall of man, is still available to us today.

- Satan came and tempted Adam and Eve by appealing to them to exercise their self-will by disobeying God and His instruction to not eat of the tree of the knowledge of "Good and Evil"; and that if they did, they would surely die. They did go to "self" and ate of the tree, and surely did die – they lost the Spirit which was resident in them. They handed over to Satan the authority of the earth that had been given to them by God; and as a result, Satan gained control over the world with an operation of destruction – kill, steal and destroy – entropy

adversity

where everything is going to decay, and finally, destruction. So, with sinful, selfish mankind living on earth and operating as a sophisticated animal with self-centered decisions and the earth becoming a place of destruction, our life is going to experience trouble, tribulation, difficulty, annoyance, hardship, oppression, bad things happening – adversity. It is now normal, and until Christ returns, is also irreversible. We live in enemy territory and cannot escape the difficult place we live in.

- God provided another way. He brought His new Kingdom where He can restore His original plan – the exceptional life – to those who believe and walk in what He has provided. Through Christ's redemptive work at the cross, where He took the penalty for the deserved punishment for sin we were given back the authority that was lost by mankind to Satan. Those who believe (and are born again and have the Spirit reenter their life) now have the opportunity to overcome the destructive world we live in and have Christ restore to us His original plan of the exceptional, abundant life. Thus, we live in two kingdoms – the Kingdom of God which is superior in power and might; and the kingdom of earth that is still controlled by Satan with the nature of destruction and entropy. As believers, we have the choice to "walk in the Spirit" and operate in His Kingdom, under His rulership, leading and guiding, and under His supernatural work in, through and around us; or, we can live in the carnal (self) and leave the Kingdom life and be subject to the kingdom of the world and all its destruction – and will surely experience adversity. It is our choice (Deuteronomy 30:11–20): We can choose Him and walk in the Kingdom where there is life and blessing; or by not choosing Him and not walking in the Kingdom, we experience death and curses. Since we live in the two kingdoms with its exceptional life of God, in the middle of enemy territory with its destructive forces, we are to understand that adversity is always present. It should not surprise us that adversity will impact our lives, even as we are living in the Kingdom and experiencing His exceptional life for us.

Furthermore, God's truth stands on its own. Those who are self-seeking and do not seek nor pursue the truth will experience God's indignation and wrath, and we will all experience tribulation and anguish. So, a global system, and/or a nation that turns its back on God will suffer greater and greater trouble. None of us who are in this global system and/or nation (unbelievers, Spirit filled believers and carnal believers) are exempt. We in America lived even in the last 30 years, a protected life from abnormal adversity, but no longer. The level of adversity will

adversity

increase and become normal.

The key is to understand the nature of adversity, the different causes of adversity and then our responses to the adversity in these difference scenarios.

section 2
UNDERSTANDING CAUSES OF ADVERSITY AND GOD'S DESIRE FOR OUR RESPONSE TO THIS ADVERSITY

We were leading a retreat in Texas in January 2014 on "Overcoming & Deliverance - the Life of David." The first night a woman stated that her life was disappointing and that God was the cause of her disappointing life, since everything that happens is God's will (this frame of thought is called Christian fatalism). So, the Lord said for me to go ahead and take a diversion to address this. Just that morning, I was teaching at the CEO Forum Spiritual Leadership Institute with Richard Blackaby, and this same question came up. I taught as I had understood it. After I sat down, the Father spoke to me that I only partially understood and there was much more to understand, and HE gave me the revelation of the much more on the spot. I wrote it all down. When this woman asked

adversity

the same question, the Lord spoke, "Here you go, teach what I gave you this morning."

As I was speaking it, the Spirit just flowed, and all that I had learned including where to go in the Scripture was revealed. It was all brand new to me, and I just let it flow, not really speaking anything from existing knowledge. This answers a lot of questions about adversity and negative circumstances, which is a struggle for a lot of Christians. On Sunday when the group was sharing, the woman apologized for diverting the group. I then shared what had happened since my time of teaching on Friday morning with Blackaby and assured her that this was from God for me and for the group. She did say that when I was teaching this on Friday night, there was a spiritual glow coming from me, and she knew that something was up. Yes, that something was the Spirit. Wow!

Here is what we have received on this: First, most Christians are living in a deep sense of "Christian fatalism," where they believe that everything that happens is God's will and that all of the adversity that comes against us is ordained by God and intended to teach us lessons and help us get stronger. This actually keeps us in a place of accepting the adversity as normal, and developing a life of disappointment and resignation. Further, it perpetuates staying in the adversity, since if this is my lot in life, because God has ordained it, I cannot do anything about it anyway and should accept it. As my heart goes deeper into thinking God is not really that good (as evidenced by my continual difficult circumstances), then I do not care much about being in His Word, not learning the true remedies available to me to release these adversities and to live in the wonder and awe of God's Kingdom.

As outlined above, Adam and Eve, during their time in the Garden of Eden before the fall, did not experience any adversity. Also, at the end of time as we know it, God creates a new heaven and a new earth where all translated believers live. We are organized into nations and governments and will have "physicality" in an eternal existence that is progressive and very stimulating. There again, we will have no adversity. So, adversity exists because of the fall (earth under entropy where everything is going to destruction) and the selfish nature of mankind, where others have the power and means to come against us and cause us trouble in our everyday life. There are multiple causes of adversity and our understanding of these in our specific situations is crucial to how we respond to these adversities, and live out the abundant life for which Christ came and promised to give us:

chapter 4
GENERAL ADVERSITY

We all (unbelievers, spirit-filled believers, and carnal believers) live in a fallen world. Jesus, when he ended His upper room discourse to the disciples, and before His final prayer to the Father, and then moving to His battle in Gethsemane, spoke these words (John 16:33): "These things I have spoken to you, that in Me you may have peace. In the world you will have tribulation; but be of good cheer, I have overcome the world." Because we all live in this fallen world, a world of entropy where everything is going to decay and destruction, we will encounter general trouble and tribulation. We are not exempt just because we are living in the Kingdom of God. We still exist in two kingdoms at once. Trouble and tribulation are everywhere and are pervasive. It covers us all – everyone and everything. Why? Because we are casualties of the fall and the effect of the fall. Our world is characterized by difficulty, frustration, annoyance, pain, hardship, struggle, oppression, etc. – things not working well, and all things are going to destruction. We are caught right in the middle of this, and everything around us in our everyday lives is working against our desires of righteousness, peace and joy. Things just are not going to work over time; and what we expect for our businesses, marriages, families, ministries, etc. just are going to face opposition and trouble. "In the world you will have tribulation." As a spirit-filled believer living in the Kingdom of God, we are not immune to this general trouble; it is not directed to me personally but happens generally. It should not surprise us that we encounter trouble, and must realize that it just there – all around me are encountering this as well, and it is not directed toward me specifically by either God or Satan. It is the nature of our world. As an example, several years ago here in Colorado, we received a snowstorm that dumped over 75 inches of snow in a 24-hour period. When we opened the front door of our house, the snow was above the door frame and we could not exit the house. The snowstorm did not just come against our house, but everywhere throughout the front-range in Colorado. Everyone experienced the same general adversity. Another example is when Linda and I go to a restaurant and because several of the servers did not show up, our service is poor. This is not directed to us specifically, but all of us in that restaurant are experiencing the same general adversity. Our car will break down; our air conditioner will break down; the wood on

adversity

our house will decay; the dishwasher will fail; the traffic lights will all be red and, I will be late; the plane will have mechanical problems, and I will miss my connection; the sale that I thought would happen for my business and was all ready to go will be canceled, because some difficult thing happened to the buyer, etc., etc. This also includes disease, sickness, illness, deformity, disabilities, and injuries. We live in a fallen world that has disease, sickness, illness, deformity, disabilities and injuries. None of us are truly exempt, especially when it's the consequences of lousy eating and exercise habits, of being exposed to viruses or living in filthy conditions where bacteria thrives. These things will impact all of us, even believers. This is one of the reasons why all believers are not instantly healed. We are part of a world that has disease, sickness, illness, deformity, disabilities, and injuries. They are not caused specifically by God, nor are they a specific attack of Satan; rather, it is part of our general adversity caused by the consequences of living in a fallen world where these types of things are normal and always present. God has not intervened in this natural course of events that brings disease, sickness, illness, deformity, disabilities and injuries. It happens at some level to all of us (including believers), and some more severe than others, not because God chose them to experience the consequences of these, but rather we experience the consequences because of the condition of a decaying and destructive world under the influence of Satan.

General adversity is real, is always there, and covers us all. It does not have any specific purpose by God or by Satan against me, but rather is characteristic of our fallen nature and world. It just is.

Response

As spirit-filled believers, we are to remain in the Kingdom and stay in His peace. We are to understand that this is just general adversity, common to many, because we are living in the fallen world. We are not to allow this to irritate or frustrate us. His peace is within us, and we can live out that peace in this situation. Further, we are to ask for wisdom regarding any move we need to make regarding this general adversity, since it does affect us now. When we encountered the snowstorm, we asked for wisdom about what to do. The Father told us to shovel the snow off the deck, since it will collapse it from its weight. As we were shoveling the snow of the deck (it took two hours), we heard the cracking of branches from evergreens that had been planted a few years before. We again asked for wisdom, and the Father told us to go out and brush off the snow from the trees or we would lose them. Linda tied a rope to my waist; and I literally swam through the snow to the trees with a broom and brushed off the snow. After coming back in, the Lord told us that we weren't going anywhere for three days, so just enjoy the fellowship of the family with games, reading, DVDs, and more importantly, abiding deeper in the Word and in prayer. We did not lose our

adversity

peace, did not let this frustrate us, and further, thoroughly enjoyed our time together in a situation that completely shut down our plans for the week. In the restaurant scenarios, we remain in peace, and specifically ask for wisdom from the Father regarding what to do. In one situation at the airport, the poor service was delaying our meal and was going to cause us to miss our plane, so after not having been served for fifteen minutes, the Lord told us to get up and go to another take-out restaurant at the airport and take the food on the plane. In another situation, we were at an expensive restaurant prior to attending a play. The poor service was causing delay, and it seemed likely that just to finish, we would be late to the play. The Father told us to tell the waiter that we had no time for dessert and to ask for the bill when the entrée came. We made the play in plenty of time and did not lose our peace throughout the entire evening. In other situations, the Father told us to relax and enjoy the fellowship throughout the longer than expected meal, as we had experienced in Europe, many times. There, it is normal for a meal to last 2 to 3 hours, and we use the relaxed atmosphere to have sweet and meaningful communications. God said, this is one of those times, and enjoy it to the full. We did and did not lose our peace. When things break down like air conditioners and dishwashers, we stay in peace, call a repair man, and if the price to fix it is too high, we just replace it. If necessary, we can live with the consequences of being hot or doing dishes by hand (and of course it always happens when you have a big gathering!). **Note, in order to live well in this** *world of general adversity, it is important to be living out the truths of God in our lives. For example, He says we are to tithe and then save, so that He can bless us with financial freedom and give us the means to be able to pay for the repair or the replacement. If we have savings, we are fully able to handle the general adversity of things breaking down (because they will), without resorting to anger and frustration, because we have no funds to take care of it. Further, God will make things last longer which blesses us even more.*

When we experience disease, sickness, illness, deformity, disabilities and injuries, we may need to consider that this may just be the consequence of general adversity and not an adversity against me specifically. We are not to go to fatalism ("Oh well, I guess this is my lot in life.") or the other direction and think, "If only I had enough faith, God would heal me." Rather, we are to ask the Father His will for this adversity, how He wishes to glorify Himself through this and what are His plans for us living out His promised abundant life. In John 9:5, Jesus was asked about a man born blind from birth and whether it was his parents or him who sinned that caused the blindness. Jesus spoke: "Neither, but that the works of God should be revealed in Him." It was general adversity that many experience and is not caused by any particular sin. As Jesus was there, He now wanted to heal him to reveal The Father's glory. God is a healer and wants to heal, and may choose to deal with our general adversity in a different way, one that will glorify Him, while He brings us the exceptional life still

adversity

available to us. I was born with a deformity of the hip ball and socket called Perthese Disease. I was a superb athlete and possibly good enough to make it in professional baseball as a pitcher. We went undefeated two years in a row in an advanced league, and before I was slated as the starting pitcher for the state all-star game, my parents and I discovered this hip disease. My sports days were over. I had to go on crutches for a year and could never again play at that level of sports. It would have been too dangerous in possibly damaging the hip further and even not being able to walk. It was painful, and I lived with this pain for 40+ years. I did not think it was God singling me out or even a specific attack of the enemy. It just happened, because we live in a fallen, destructive world. I desired to be healed, and I was learning about the power of God and His supernatural work of healing. I thought like so many that I was not being healed, because I just did not have enough faith. The Lord spoke to me that this was part of general adversity, to live with it and wait for the right time for healing. He also spoke that I should not think it cannot involve medicine and doctors and that they were part of his healing process and that I shouldn't care about the way I would be healed. A CEO friend of mine, Tim Sotos, encouraged me to check the new technology with an orthopedic specialist. I did and he said the technology had become so good that it would now outlive me, and he encouraged me to have surgery. The Father said yes. I had the hip replacement and immediately was relieved of the life-long pain (and my golf game got better). The surgeon said the bone material would take a year to

SECTION 2

grow into the implant for it to be fully functional. At my one month checkup, the hip was x-rayed, and the surgeon came to the my exam room and said he had never experienced this in all the 5,000 surgeries he had done. My bone was completely filled in to the implant – he even said it was a miracle. It was. God had an answer to this general adversity – live with it, wait, and let me direct you to healing. He did not cause it, but had the power to resolve it and give me the wisdom to understand it.

The key to this all is to stay in peace, ask for wisdom and to not allow this general adversity and often very frustrating situation affect God's plans for us today. It is actually a wonderful opportunity to bear witness to the life of the Spirit in us, as we can remain at peace, be kind and respectful, and stand out against all the others who show their frustration with anger, demanding their way and hurtful words. We are called to be different and respond to the general adversity that brings frustration with the nature of Christ in us.

chapter 5
TEST OF FAITH

God tells us in James chapter 1:2–5: "my brethren, count it all joy when you fall into various trials, knowing that the testing of your faith produces patience. But let patience have its perfect work, that you may be perfect and complete, lacking nothing. If any of you lacks wisdom, let him ask of God, who gives to all liberally and without reproach, and it will be given to him." There are trials and tribulations that are orchestrated directly by God but purely as a test of faith. This will occur only to Christians who are abiding and hearing what promises or truths The Father is speaking to us personally. Faith is defined in Hebrews 11:1 as "the substance of things hoped for, the evidence (or certainty) of things not seen." The only things that we can be certain of that are not seen are what God speaks. He further tells us in Hebrews 11:6 that "without faith, it is impossible to please Him," which means that our entire life will be challenged with opportunities for faith. We can never get to a point where we have so orchestrated our life that we don't need faith, since it is impossible to please Him without it. Further, He tells us in Hebrews 12:1–2: "let us lay aside every weight, and the sin which so easily ensnares us, and let us run with endurance, the race that is set before us, looking unto Jesus, the author and finisher of our faith, who for the joy that was set before Him endured the cross, despising the shame, and sat down at the right hand of the throne of God." Christ authors by speaking His promises and truths to us, and then finishes it (to the point that we have certainty that His promise will be fulfilled.). To finish it, we must be tested solely for the purpose of us knowing whether what He has spoken is certain to us. We would not know unless the adversity (trial) that He brings is tested.

We know that we pass the test when we do not go to fear, anxiety, worry, trying to figure out Plan B; but rather, we are at complete peace and have settled in our heart that though this trial has come against us and is opposite of what God's promise has spoken, we know with certainty that it will happen. We will be able to say from a true heart, the same thing that David came to when he passed the trial of faith in 2 Samuel 7:28 and 29: "and now, O Lord God, you are God, and Your words are true, and You promised this goodness to your servant. Now, therefore, let it please You to bless us… For You, O Lord God, have spoken it, and with Your blessing, let the house of Your servant be blessed forever." The trial is meant not to harm us but rather to reveal to us that we are not yet finished. We cannot just say we believe; we have to be tested to prove our faith. And we know from Romans 10:17 that "faith comes from hearing and hearing from the Word (Rhema – what the Father is speaking from Logos - Promises and Truth - to us personally). Thus, the only time we will experience this type of trial will be when we are in the process of hearing what God is speaking to us in the Word, and then by abiding in the Word allow Him to finish taking His Word to faith. If we are not abiding and not hearing His promises, there is no trial being initiated by God, since we have not even had Christ author faith, as we have not heard His promise or truth to us. The trial will only be long enough for us to have faith finished by Christ's work through our abiding.

Response

We are to fully cooperate with this adversity. We are not to ask The Father to remove the adversity, since this would counteract His purpose of finishing our faith. Rather, we are to go deeper into the abiding, and dialogue with The Father as to why we are responding to this trial with fear, anxiety, worry, and trying to figure out Plan B. We need to understand the wounds and patterns of our life that God is working to transform and fulfill His wonderful plans for us. We are not to see the adversity as something to be fought, oppressed by or rejected, but rather to be embraced. We must understand its purpose and know that we are to be delivered through it and not from it. We are to ask the Father to reveal all that he desires so that we will go to faith, and thus have this trial ended. As Linda and I are receiving God's promises and truths, we normally see things get worse at first. We know that we are in His trial to test our faith and realize we are not to pray against this adversity, but to go deeper in our abiding in Him. For one of our investment properties, the Lord had spoken a promise to us that He wanted us to sell it, and He would provide above market price (in a down market when not much was selling). He had confirmed this with Scripture to trust Him and be persuaded that he would fulfill what he had promised (Romans 4:21). Having heard His instruction and confirming it through unity together with the Spirit, we put the property up for sale. For two months we had few showings and prices around us, continued to drop. The worsening situation was a test of faith - were we going to let circumstances discourage us and have us go to resignation? (Yes, we failed a few times during these two months). We knew that this was a test of faith and not to ask God to fix it or to go to fatalism and just believe that we didn't hear correctly. We both had to abide deeper in His word about trust in what was spoken to us. Though we were failing this test of faith, we were to stay with Him and let Him finish. Our realtor, a good friend, actually had faith, and believed with us that it was going to sell at our asking price; and not drop the price or just give up on it. In the

adversity

third month after we had passed the test, a buyer came and paid full price. It was a lengthy process from offer to closing, as the buyer needed to sell their property, and we had to receive faith for that as well (which we again failed a few times during that period). During this process, the faith that Christ authored was finished. He did reconfirm His promise when we were doubting, walked us through the adversity of negative circumstances when we failed the test, and finished His faith in us, as we abided and were transformed by His work. One thing we fully understood was that we could not flip things on God by asking him to prove His promise in order for us to believe. That puts us in the self, acting as God, which He will not allow. In fact, this limits His ability to act (Psalm 78:40–42). He says quite the opposite – that in order for Him to fulfill His promise, we must go to faith (certainty in what He has spoken) by letting Him finish it through testing and the transforming work in our hearts. And, He can wait longer than we can. It is best to cooperate and let Him finish our faith.

chapter 6
PRUNING

This is entirely God's work, and is intended to cut back our activities and involvements, so that His desired fruit is produced. We, by becoming too involved and burdened by too many things to do, wind up having little or no fruit. Thus, God will allow adversity in what we are doing, so that we realize we are doing too much; and need to let him rearrange our life and create space and margin for us to receive the needed sunlight (the Son) and needed water (the Holy Spirit) to enjoy being a branch and producing high quality, much (but not too much) fruit.

In February 2014, we conducted a leader's retreat in wine country, Santa Rosa, California. We visited a boutique "Zinfandel" vineyard where the owners are Christians and friends of Neal and Kathy Weisenberger (who arranged our tasting). The owners took us on a tour of the vineyard, and

adversity

we learned amazing new revelation about Abiding and more depth of Jesus' Words in John 15:1–5. Linda and I were overwhelmed by this new understanding and are still processing it all:

1. **Pruning** (cutting back growth of the branch that is getting too big to produce fruit):

    a. Only healthy branches that are capable of bearing fruit are pruned. Unless pruned properly, pruning can actually cause the branch to die and have to be discarded; and only the vinedresser knows how to do it. Each branch is individual, so there is no one system for all branches. If pruned too much or too little, there will be no fruit. It has to be exactly what is needed for that particular branch. To protect from expected adversity (less than normal rain, potential frost, heat, wind, etc.), the location of the pruning is exact, so as to allow the branch to survive the adversity. Again, only the vinedresser knows this, and if not done properly, this incorrect pruning will result in the branch dying – not because of too little or too much, but because it's done in the wrong location. **Key Revelation: Only the Vinedresser (The Father) knows exactly how much and where to prune. If we try to do this ourselves, or allow others to do this who are not the Vinedresser (churches, pastors, advisors, friends, spouses, etc.),**

we will make mistakes and actually accelerate our becoming useless and bearing no fruit.

b. The pruning has to be such that the branches and the leaves that will come and be continually pruned must have plenty of sun (SON) and water (HOLY SPIRIT) to be able to thrive. If, after the initial pruning, it starts to get too big (crowding as it flourishes, particularly in the center of the vine), it blocks the sunlight and water from the branches. Then as they get too big (although they are actually very healthy), the overgrowth then diminishes their ability to receive what is needed to thrive, and they shrink and then do not produce fruit.

c. After the initial pruning, the branches grow "shoots" from which the grapes ultimately are created and grow in bunches. As these shoots begin to grow, the vinedresser immediately prunes (just after they pop out) these shoots so that there is plenty of space for the sunlight and water. The pruning, both initially and as the branch grows itself and sprouts shoots, is required to provide plenty of open space for the sunlight and rain to reach the branches, the leaves, and soak into the dirt for strength of the vine. **Key Revelation: Pruning is ongoing, and is geared to create space for sunlight and water, which are the sources of**

adversity

life. This is in addition to the primary reason of having the branch not get so big that the sap can't get through the branch into the fruit and so that water (Holy Spirit) is not absorbed by the branch resulting in no fruit. The Covenant: Blessed to become a blessing by giving it away. WE NEED SPACE and MARGIN. Our abiding is to fully allow, cooperate with, and desire the Father to prune back our activities (all the stuff we are doing), so that we can receive plenty of the Son and the Holy Spirit to produce His desired fruit. Without this space, the growth that seems really good to us (and measured as good by the world and even by the church) actually causes us to dry up, wither and have no fruit. This describes us so well in becoming weary, worn out, even burned out with our good activities. We all need to pay attention to this. A big invitation by The Father to cut back, cut back, cut back. Do not think it disappointing God or selfish. On the contrary, it is His perfect will for the fruit He plans and desires.

2. Fruit: This one caught us by surprise. **If the fruit (bunches of grapes) from the branches is so much that it touches each other, they rot, become mushy and are worthless.** This "touching of bunches of grapes" does not allow the air needed for the grapes to continue its proper completion; and through this lack of air, they cause each other to rot. The fruit also needs space or it becomes worthless. **Key revelation: We always thought that much fruit meant as much fruit as possible, and isn't that a good thing. Not so. When the fruit gets too much, it causes all of what's on that branch to rot. Wow, even the fruit needs to be managed and given plenty of space! Thus, we are not in any way to view the magnitude of our fruit as our responsibility or think that more is better. Rather, it is about what the Vinedresser desires, and trusting that He knows what is optimal for us. Our fruit is to be discrete, and thus, not all forced together making it seem even bigger. Further, the fruit is individual, so having large groups where there is no space for the fruit to thrive causes the very fruit produced to rot and be worthless. This means to us that we will not actually know the fruit that God brings forth through our being faithful and just abiding, but by allowing Him to prune and bring His desired fruit. We believe this speaks to multiplication and that our real ministry "fruit" is helping those who God brings across our path to experience us receiving the amazing fruit of transformation and supernatural work. They themselves then want to get connected to the Vine and learn to abide, as well as experience the lessons of pruning through space and margin.**

adversity

It is a big reorientation of our role, our willingness to let The Father prune us for this space and margin, and understand that the very fruit of those who become fruit is produced for them to get connected with others and enjoy the life of abiding. This is very profound, but not easy to grasp.

Response

Completely cooperate with this adversity - and the sooner the better. His pruning is always ongoing. We will experience less and easier adversity, if we pay attention to His pruning and allow Him to complete it. Because healthy branches grow and naturally get bigger, it is critical that they be pruned to produce fruit. Thus, this is not something that occurs once in a while, but all the time, since our inclination as we grow is to get more active and more involved in things, especially good things. We have to understand that these good things may not be God's things, and that the only things that matter are God's things. Since we understand pruning is completely from the vinedresser - (The Father) Linda and I work to cooperate fully and allow Him to prune us. We sit down quarterly and review all the new activities and involvements that have grown naturally into our lives. We hold sacred the most important activities of personal abiding, abiding as a couple, abiding as a family, personal time together as a couple and with family, Sabbath, holidays and time off as a couple and with family (building exceptional memories), balanced work, and then God's ministry assignment for us. Anything new that has already come in as a result of natural growth or is being presented to us now, we evaluate before God. If this new activity or involvement is from God, then by definition, He has to instruct us what has to come off. And we know that the most important activities mentioned above cannot be diminished or sloughed. For sure, this would mean we would experience no fruit, since without Him, we can do nothing. So, abiding is critical and it is our priority. We fully cooperate with God's wisdom, even with the new things that have come up within our ministry assignment. For example, Linda and I were leading numerous "beginning" abiding retreats and other general retreats, through the Living Waters ministry; and we were working to build leaders, so that the ministry might be multiplied according to God's instructions to us. As we evaluated our involvements, God spoke that we needed to significantly reduce our beginning abiding retreats, do no more general retreats, and replace these with leader retreats. It became clear how we were to alter our activities and allow Him to prune us. We did not attempt to just keep adding more and more, thinking that this would have been better and more fruitful. We soon realized that it is best to fully cooperate with God's pruning. Further, we also recognize that our capacities for involvements and activities are not the same. Linda cannot handle as many plates as me. Thus, we both have to understand when one of us has reached God's limits of our individual plates. Our awareness comes in the form of stress, weariness, and being tired. We help each other when we

adversity

notice that the other is experiencing these. When Linda is stressed and weary, it is clear that she is loaded up with too many activities and involvements at the moment (usually caused by me). As we recognize this, I help her to clear her calendar completely and take 2 to 3 days off to spend some re-energizing time with God alone. This is usually at her prayer mountain, where she is able to resettle and re-center; and then we work to rearrange our activities in our calendar so that her plates are back in balance. For all of us, it is an ongoing thing. Fully cooperate with His pruning. It is entirely for our benefit and for producing His fruit. HIS fruit, not ours or other people's. It keeps us in the wonderful place of peace and joy, contentment and relaxed emotions. Why would we ever not fully cooperate with this?

chapter 7
SELF-CENTEREDNESS

In James 1:12–18, The Word tells us: "the man endures temptation; for when he has been approved, he will receive the crown of life which the Lord has promised to those who love them. Let no one say when he is tempted, I am tempted by God; for God cannot be tempted by evil, nor does He Himself tempt anyone. But each one is tempted when he is drawn away by His own desires and enticed. Then, when desire has conceived, it gives birth to sin; and sin, when it is full-grown, brings forth death. Do not be deceived, my beloved brethren. Every good gift and every perfect gift is from above, and comes down from the Father of lights, with whom there is no variation or shadow of charge. Of His own will, He brought us forth by the Word of Truth, that we might be a kind of first fruits of His creatures." Isaiah 59: 1–2 says, "behold, the

adversity

Lord's hand is not shortened, that it cannot save; nor is it heavy, that it cannot hear. But your iniquities have separated you from your God; and your sins have hidden His face from you, so that He will not hear." In essence, adversity can come because we follow our selfish desire (our own agenda, our own decisions, and not checking in with the Father). We are drawn away from the Kingdom of God where we are protected, and given favor (read all of Psalm 91); and we walk out into the world (the enemy's Kingdom), which is a destructive place. When we choose our own way, we sin and miss the mark; and if we do not repent quickly, this sin brings forth death, which is the separation from the life of the spirit, and thus, the power and protection of God. It is important to know that God does not tempt us in any way and is not partial, but rather that He offers every good gift to all of us who are willing to walk in the spirit with Him in His Kingdom, where the favor and the abundant life resides. When we no longer experience protection and favor, things don't work too well, and adversity naturally comes against us. We experience more and more difficulties, and we are thwarting our receiving the planned blessings from God. As a result, we feel as though we're rolling a boulder uphill. Since God in no way has brought this adversity against us, we cannot blame Him, nor expect Him to remove it. Because it is self-through our self-will and walking away from the blessed place – we are choosing the awful, oppressive place of the enemy whose world is hard and difficult. The only remedy is repentance. God is asking us, "How is that working out for you?" Then, He invites us to repent and come back into His Kingdom and into relationship again with him. Remember, the Kingdom of God is always just a step away. Having truly repented (turned 180 degrees from self to follow Him), we then can boldly ask the Father to eliminate the adversity, even though we have caused it ourselves. That is the beauty of His sovereignty and love for us. He does not condemn us (Romans 8: 1–2), but says "welcome back, take my hand and let's go forward in my Kingdom, according to my plan for you, which is abundant life and favor." After Joshua experienced the amazing battle of Jericho where the walls fell because he followed God's instruction, he decided to attack a small nearby city, Ai. He did not check in with the Father, but rather decided on His own that he could easily handle this attack. He was soundly defeated, as he walked into enemy territory without the protection and favor of God. He knew he did not have a right to complain, nor did he ask God to defeat the enemy. What he did do was repent. He recognized that he had forgotten to check in and understood that through His selfish desires, he gave birth to sin and walked away from the protection and favor of God, experiencing the adversity naturally there in the world. It did not go well with him, and he recognized it. Upon repentance, God told him that had he checked in, God would have spoken that there was sin in the camp that needed to be dealt with and before he could go further, He would have instructed Joshua to locate the sin and eliminate this sin caused by a clan disobeying the instruction of God regarding the taking of certain items from Jericho. After Joshua fulfilled God's instruction about the sin, God told him to go back to Ai, as now, with God's favor and protection, the enemy will be defeated; and it was. This is a clear picture that the defeat was not God's will and was not caused by God. Rather, it was caused by selfishness and the consequences of walking away from the Kingdom of God: hardship, difficulty, and oppression; and upon the repentance and reconnecting with God, the adversity ceased and victory won.

Response

As with Joshua, the remedy is simple – repentance. We are called to recognize that our selfishness has carried us away from God, and that the adversity we are experiencing is not from God, but from the natural destructive forces of the world. They are hard and not pleasant. God has given us clear indicators that we have followed self and walked away from Him - these are the absence of righteousness, peace, and joy in the Holy Spirit (Romans 14:17), freedom (2Cor. 3:17), and forgiveness (Mark 11:25). He desires that these indicators become so sensitive, that we immediately know when they are not present that we have walked away from the Kingdom; and that the remedy is simply repentance and return back to Him immediately, allowing Him to lead us according to

SECTION 2

His will and His plan for us. If we don't, the adversity is not released and we continue to live in difficulty and things not going well. God does not force us to repent; rather, He invites us to understand that it is much better living with Him in His Kingdom than on our own, outside of His Kingdom. In this scenario, we have no right to ask Him to release the adversity until we repent, return back into fellowship with him in His Kingdom, and walk with him. Then He will give us instruction that will lead us to the adversity ceasing.

One example: Linda and I had purchased a new car (a one-year-old car, which is the best value). We had some extra options put on this car and had to wait several days for it to be completed. When Linda received the car, she noticed that there apparently was some damage to the car and refused to accept it. She came home and told me that something had happened, and that she did not feel good about this car at all. She said that I should tell them that we were not taking the car and asked me to look for another one. I called the car dealer, and he said that someone had just become too aggressive with polishing and waxing and that they would be able to take care of it, no big deal. Linda said no. I said, "We've already got the paperwork all done, and they have our check, so it will be fine." It wasn't. In a few weeks, the entire front panel fell off, several holes were in the bottom of the car, and the windows whistled with air coming through. Linda took the car to a body shop, and they told her that the entire car had been damaged and most everything except the doors had been replaced, including the top. They suspected that while the car was on the lift to

adversity

install the options, it fell off and was completely damaged. I called the dealer, and he said, "Tough, sue us." I related the story to a Christian lawyer friend who joined me in my indignation and said he would provide the legal services free of charge. Fantastic! God showing me favor, right? While I was preparing the information to go after this crooked dealer, God asked me "What are you doing?" He said that though we might win the case, it was a waste of my time and in violation of His Word (which I knew in my heart). He said, "This consequence and adversity is because you did not check in with me, did not go in unity with your wife as you teach others, and thought you could handle it." He invited me to repent and to return back into His Kingdom and back into an intimate relationship with him. I did and then, ah, decided it would be good to check in. He said go buy your wife a new car. I said, "Yeah, but this is going to cost me big time." He said, "Exactly $8,000, because you have to trade in the damaged car and tell the new dealer that it is damaged." This was an expensive lesson, and I caused the adversity completely. Upon repentance, God eliminated the adversity (though not the consequence) and gave me the freedom to forget the things that lay behind and press on to the high calling of Christ Jesus in great peace and joy. Linda forgave me and was rather happy, because she got a new car and drives it still today.

chapter 8
DISCIPLINE

If after we have operated in the self that has brought about sin and walked away from God's Kingdom, and we still have not repented and continue to reject His invitations to return, God will bring His discipline to us. Hebrews 12: 5–7 says, "And you have forgotten that exhortation speaks to you as to sons: my son, do not despise the chastening of the Lord, nor be discouraged when you are rebuked by him; for whom the Lord loves he chastens, and scourges every son whom He receives. If you endure chastening, God deals with you as with sons, for what son is there whom a father does not chasten?" Think about why discipline is necessary. It is because the stubbornness of the will has not been broken and there is a decided resistance to repentance. The child decides that he is not going to listen to the parent and do exactly what he wants, though he is experiencing harder and more difficult things at that time. The purpose of the discipline is simply to cause the child to break his will, repent, and return back to the life intended. The intensifying of the adversity is from God. It is purposeful. It will not be released until we exercise the only remedy – repentance, as described above in chapter 7 on self-centeredness. Again, without repentance we have no right to complain and no right to ask God to remove the adversity, as this is from Him and will continue until we repent. A good example of this is the Israelites after they crossed the Red Sea. God spoke a promise to them, that He would give them the Promised land, which was spectacular and where they would experience the abundant life. Through their self-centeredness, they refused to go, and walked away from following God and experiencing His blessings. He was angry with them for 40 years (Heb 3:15-19), and their hardships became more difficult and more oppressive. They never repented, and they experienced the discipline of God their entire lives. What was even sadder was that they did not receive any more promises, since the next promise is contingent on us following Him and receiving the promise set before us.

Response:

Repentance. Upon repentance, God's discipline will stop (the only reason for the adversity is to get us to repent), and we can boldly ask Him to remove any adversity that has been caused by our self-centeredness. Again, no matter

SECTION 2

how big of a pickle we have put ourselves into, God can take care of it all, since nothing is too difficult for Him. Interestingly enough, as things become more difficult, we have a tendency to get angry at God and actually move further away from repentance. Romans 8:5–8 tells us that there are three consequences to walking in the flesh (self-centeredness): death of the spirit (disconnected and not operating); enmity against God; and inability to please God. These consequences caused us to lose the protection and favor of God (as described above), and are enmity - actually working against the will of God that would take us to the blessed life. As we experience God's discipline where the adversity is intensified, our thinking tends to flip completely. We think that God is at enmity against us and working to harm us. If God would only stop this adversity, I would think that He loves me again, and I would be willing to walk with Him again. This perverse thinking only serves to accentuate the discipline, since it causes us to develop even harder hearts that makes it more difficult to repent. When things are so bad, our best response is to recognize that we are under God's discipline and the best remedy is to repent, return to His loving relationship, begin again to abide in Him, and be restored back to the abundant life where the adversities from this cause will stop. As a young executive of a Fortune 500 company, I was advised to invest in real estate where large equity gains were available. I did, and my first project was wildly successful. It took all of the equity and invested it in three more projects. Linda had strongly urged me that this was not God's will

adversity

and not to proceed. Because of my self-centeredness, I ignored her and started these three projects. Many things began to not work well, and the adversity intensified. A deep recession hit, and I was unable to maintain the required loan payments of the projects. I was in trouble. I was being disciplined but did not think it necessary to repent. We never do when we think we are doing right, which is purely pride. As a result, it got more and more oppressive, even as I was asking God to solve the problem. When He didn't, I felt that He was against me and wondered where was the good God that I had known before? I'll tell you more of this story in the next section.

chapter 9
JUDGEMENT

After the natural adversity caused by self-centeredness, it's then intensified through God's discipline, and finally comes God's judgment. If we have not responded in repentance to the discipline, God brings such a severe consequence in the form of judgment until we are completely broken. Jeremiah 1:16 says, "I will utter my judgments against them concerning all their wickedness, because they have forsaken me, burned incense to other gods, and worshiped the works of their own hands." Jeremiah 7: 24–26, 30, 34 says, "Yet they do not obey or incline your ear, but followed the counsels and the dictates of their evil hearts, and went backward and not forward....Yet they did not obey me, or incline their ear, but stiffened their neck. They were worse than their Fathers....The children of Judah have done evil in my sight says the Lord. They have set their abominations

adversity

in My house, which is called by My name to pollute it ... Therefore, I will cause to cease from the cities of Judah from the streets of Jerusalem the voice of mirth and the voice of gladness, the voice of the bridegroom and the voice of the bride. For the land shall be desolate." The people of Israel had walked away from the blessed life of God - through their own self-centeredness - and were experiencing the natural adversity as a consequence. Since they did not repent, God brought discipline and intensified the adversity. For thirteen years, Jeremiah, as God's prophet, invited them to avoid further discipline and repent. They refused and continued to develop harder hearts. As a result, God warned them that He would bring judgment - the destruction of the nation, the city and the Temple, by the Babylonians. The judgment was so severe that those who refused to follow God's instructions were all killed in the battle. The only ones to survive were those who repented at the judgment and became part of the remnant – they enjoyed a good life provided by God, though in a different country where their former life was lost. They did have consequences to their choices. Isaiah 9:6 says, "For unto us a child is born, for unto us a child is given. And the government will be upon His shoulder. And His name will be called Wonderful Counselor, Almighty God, Everlasting Father, Prince of Peace. Of the increase of His government and peace there will be no end and... To order it and establish it with judgment and justice from that time forward, even forever." We must understand that God's rule, His government, His Kingdom includes judgment. Why? Because in addition to being Loving and Compassionate, He is Holy. And His holiness is represented by His Word (His Truth). John 12:46–50 tells us, "I have come as light into the world, that whoever believes in me should not abide in darkness. If anyone hears my words, and does not believe, I do not judge him for I did not come to judge the world, but to save the world. He who rejects me and does not receive my words, has that which judges him – the Word that I have spoken will judge him in the last day. For I have not spoken on my own authority, but the Father who sent me, gave me a command, what I should say what I should speak, and I know that His command is everlasting life. Therefore, whatever I speak just as the Father has told me. So, I speak". His words stand on their own because they are truth. He has not come to judge, but rather we are judged by His words. If we have not repented because of our self-centeredness, and if we have not repented at His discipline, His truth brings judgment. God realizes that there is nothing left through intense adversity of His discipline that will cause us to repent, except a severe judgment that breaks us. Even then it is to bring us to repentance and to restore us to the abundant life that He promises. At that moment, though we have experienced a most severe consequence, He can restore us back to the exceptional life promised. As described above under Discipline, my heart had gotten harder and

adversity

I did not respond to God's intense discipline of adversity. Finally, His truth brought judgment and we lost everything, having to file chapter 7 Bankruptcy forced by the banks who owned the projects. Although we had saved and had big stock gains from my work as a corporate executive, everything was lost. Even my cars were taken away. We literally had nothing. The judgment was so severe that I finally broke. I repented and surrendered my will to His. He asked me if I was willing to let Him rule, let Him guide and lead me, and allow Him to give me His abundant life, as I learn to abide and follow Him. Having been broken, I said yes. Linda forgave me, and we started afresh with Him. Within three years He restored everything that we had lost and set us on a course of living a truly abundant life in the covenant - blessed to become a blessing. We learned a most valuable lesson that it was way better to repent earlier and not let hard heartedness lead to judgment. God's truth stands; and He will judge us if we refuse to repent and walk with Him.

chapter 10
ATTACK OF SATAN: CIRCUMSTANCES AGAINST US

1 Peter 5: 8 says: "Be sober, be vigilant; because your adversary the devil walks about like a roaring lion, seeking whom he may devour." The enemy is real, and is prowling constantly as an adversary against Christians, seeking to make use of every opportunity to destroy us (cause us to experience circumstances that ruin our lives, our relationships, our life with God and lead us to broken heartedness, discouragement, despair, and resignation). In Ephesians 6:10–20, the Lord tells us: "Finally, my brethren, be strong in the Lord and in the power of His might. Put on the whole armor of God; that you may be able to stand against the wiles of the devil. For we do not wrestle against flesh and blood, but against principalities, against powers, against the rulers of the darkness of this age, against spiritual

adversity

hosts of wickedness in the heavenly places. Therefore take up the whole armor of God; that you may be able to withstand in the evil day, and having done all, to stand. Stand therefore, having girded your waist with truth, having put on the breastplate of righteousness, and having shod your feet with the preparation of the gospel of peace; above all, taking the shield of faith with which you will be able to quench all the fiery darts of the wicked one. And take the helmet of salvation, and the sword of the Spirit, which is the word of God; praying always with all prayer and supplication in the Spirit, being watchful to this end with all perseverance and supplication for all the saints-- and for me, that utterance may be given to me, that I may open my mouth boldly to make known the mystery of the gospel, for which I am an ambassador in chains; that in it I may speak boldly, as I ought to speak".

We need to fully comprehend that we are targets of the enemy, who is pursing us. Thus, that the adversities and difficulties being brought by the enemy are not just natural things, but rather being driven by principalities and powers that are operating behind the scenes. These principalities and powers have the ability to use schemes or strategies to work against us. We must remember that they are created beings and not Gods. Thus, they do not have the powers of God (omniscience, omnipresence, omnipotence), but do possess powers that operate in the spiritual realm which is superior to ours in natural the realm. Since they are neither omniscient nor omnipresent, they are only capable of observing our actions and patterns. Thus, they see what causes us to be discouraged, give up, go to fear, stop abiding and walking with God, and pursue our own self-interest – which keeps us out of God's Kingdom and firmly in the kingdom of the world, where the satanic powers are superior to ours. When we are operating outside of God's Kingdom, we are no match for the principalities and powers. However, inside of God's Kingdom, the demonic powers have zero ability to influence and attack us. Thus, the enemy's strategy is to tempt us or draw us out of the Kingdom through our self-centeredness, and then to keep us out of the Kingdom – particularly by not abiding or seeking to walk with God. Through their observation, they can see patterns and thus the arrows or the stimulus of causes are done more frequently so that we fall back into that pattern. He is constantly scheming to develop strategies that bring adversity against us and cause us to fall. He usually uses other people who are captive to his influences through anger, bitterness, hardness, extreme self-centeredness, controlling, manipulating, and other perverse conditions of their hearts. They do things that come against us in our business, marriage, family, children, ministry, community, etc. They serve as roadblocks to our work, success, and enjoyment by causing negative circumstances and failure to come against us. The principalities and powers, having seen ways that draw us out of the Kingdom and prevent us from walking with God, stimulate the circumstances that are directly coming

adversity

against us – mostly using selfish people who have power and authority to cause trouble and difficulty in our circumstances. The enemy is using these selfish, manipulating, controlling people to thwart God's will for us, cause trouble, create obstacles, etc. What we thought was on track all of a sudden falls off the rails, because the enemy is attacking us through this circumstance – to destroy our plan and to destroy our heart, so we go to discouragement, fear and worry. A great example of this is Goliath and Israel. In 1 Samuel 17, the Philistines come against Israel to defeat them. They were way bigger and stronger and likely to prevail. The Philistines decide to challenge them to a single duel – their best warrior, Goliath against Israel's best warrior. Goliath states that whoever prevails, the one being defeated has to be the servant of the one prevailing. There it is. This represents Satan. His work is to prevail against us and in essence make us serve him and his work. Saul and Israel's response was to go to dismay and they were greatly afraid. They knew that based upon their own power and ability, they had no chance - same for us. If we fight the enemy in our own strength, we have no power and will be defeated, which is why his major strategy is to draw us out of the Kingdom, away from the protection and power of God, so that we attempt to fight in our own power where he has superiority, and will prevail. When this adversity comes against us, we tend to have the same response as Saul – first dismay ("Oh no, I'm in trouble and things are not going to work out."), and then we go to fear.

SECTION 2

Response

Knowing that we are fighting against principalities and powers, it is critical to understand that we can only fight against these in the spirit with God's weapons and not our natural abilities. James 4:7 says, "Therefore submit to God. Resist the devil and he will flee from you." He has to flee when we submit to God and utilize the spiritual weapons available to us, such as (Found in Ephesians 6:13):

1. **Belt of truth:** *Be willing to pursue, understand and comprehend all aspects of what is truly going on – the facts, our heart, our emotions, the spiritual dimensions, and any other truths that God wishes to reveal to us. We should be open to receiving all of this truth and not either ignoring or neglecting any of it.*

2. **Breastplate of righteousness:** *Christ is righteousness, so in order for us to put on the breastplate, we must put on Christ – be walking with Him, living in Him (abiding) and operating in His Kingdom. Without this we have no shot.*

3. **The gospel of peace on our feet:** *In order to go to battle, we must be at peace ourselves (not frustrated, worried, anxious, or fearful). Thus, this becomes a good indicator of whether we're prepared to go to battle, because we are in the right place – in His Kingdom – if*

adversity

we are at peace. Then we can proceed. If we are not at peace, then we need to stop and be restored to peace and not attempt to fight the battle on our own.

4. **The shield of faith:** *"Faith" is belief in what God has said through His word or promise about a particular battle or circumstance. So, this indicates that we would have had to ask Him what is true and then we must believe it. Thus, there may be a trial from God in the middle of this adversity, since he will test our faith - an interesting and profound truth. The shield mentioned here is not an arm shield but rather a complete body shield able to extinguish anything that the enemy can throw at us, because we will believe God and not pay attention to the cause-and-effect that the enemy is stimulating to try to bring us back to our old patterns.*

Up to this point, all of the weapons have been defensive and only operate if we are facing the battle. We are using them to protect and to quench anything that the enemy can throw at us. Now let's look at the offense and go after the enemy directly:

5. **The sword of the word:** *We now use the very promise and the truths of God to go against the enemy and to bind him and cast him out of the situation. Jesus gave us the keys to the Kingdom, which are of binding and loosing according to Matt. 16:18-19, based upon*

receiving revelation and believing it. As we receive God's Word against this attack, we can stand on it and bind up the activity of Satan and loose the power of Heaven to flood this situation. He reiterates it again in Matthew 18:18–20 and ties it to reaching agreement (unity) with another and with the Spirit, based upon what the Lord has spoken. We are standing against this attack, binding up and casting off the enemy, so that he has no power in our situation and no ability to press his strategy of killing, stealing and destroying. We stand on the truth and speak the truth that this causes the enemy to flee and not be able to accomplish his goal of thwarting God's will. We then return to God's beautiful fulfillment of our circumstances without the pressure and adversity from the enemy.

6. **Prayer:** *Throughout the process we constantly stay in prayer. We stay in fellowship with God, as we walk with Him utilizing these weapons and accomplishing the ability to stand and withstand the attack of the enemy.*

When David arrives at the battle field having been sent by his father to check up on his brothers, he sees things differently and does not go to dismay or fear. He understands that this is not a battle to be fought in the natural, which will be lost, but one to be fought with spiritual weapons. He states, "Who is this uncircumcised Philistine, that he should defy the armies of the Living

adversity

God?" He knew that Goliath had no right to be there attempting to defeat Israel since God had spoken a covenant promise to Israel, and compared to God, he was nothing. When David went to battle, he did not go in His own power, but he stated, "You come to me with a sword, with a spear, and with a javelin; but I come to you in the name of The Lord of hosts, the God of the armies of Israel, whom you have defied. This day, the Lord will deliver you into my hand, and I will strike you and take your head from you...that all the earth may know that there is a God in Israel." He used the same spiritual weapons available to us from God and proclaimed that this was God's battle, and God would win it. He stood against the enemy, because he knew that the enemy had no right to come against them; and then he took the sword of the Spirit, and in God's name and Power, the enemy was defeated and bound up. He did not just accept this adversity as, "Well, okay, I hope it goes away, or we may lose." Instead, he took his position as a follower of the Almighty God, and said, "no, you have to go." This is to be our position. We do not need to put up with this attack – the enemy has no right here and we are to understand we are not fighting flesh and blood, but principalities and powers; and they have been disarmed and defeated by Christ (Col. 2: 11–15). We do not accept this adversity, but stand and pray against it, and expect it to cease and to be overcome.

Linda and I have begun to see this more and more. When a tornado literally attacked our house in Castle Rock, Colorado, we asked God, "What do you have to say about this, and what do you want us to do?" He said, "This is the enemy directly attacking you and your family, and the ministry itself." He said that He would prevent this from harming any of us or our house; and that He wanted us to stand (literally at the door —which was glass) and pray against it. We did, and the tornado that came back to our house three times did not damage us in any way. By the way, this is all on video since the news captured it from a helicopter (Linda was the lead story on the local news that evening, giving testimony to the power of God and our belief in Christ as Lord. Surprisingly, they didn't edit one word). We knew that Satan had no right there, so how dare he defy the children and ministry of the Living God! As another example, we have experienced satanic attacks in our business. We have had people inside our clients' team (Hospital Systems) attempt to cause big difficulties by lying, manipulating and broadcasting to all the key players that we have failed at our service. First, we check the facts to understand what exactly happened. When we realize that this is lying and deception, we now know we are not fighting flesh and blood but powers and principalities – and that they have no right to defy the children and company of the Living God. We stand against it, pray the sword of the Spirit, and see it bound up and defeated. The client sees the truth, works with us to handle this situation, and our reputation actually grows. We know these attacks are from the enemy, not from God, and thus we do not need to put up with this, but stand and pray against it with full expectation that it will cease and be overcome.

chapter 11
ATTACK OF SATAN: PERSECUTION

IIn addition to the enemy coming against us with circumstances and pressures that block our path, oppress us, and work to discourage us, he specifically brings persecution against us. In Matthew 5: 10–12, Jesus tells us, "Blessed are those who are persecuted for righteousness' sake, For theirs is the kingdom of heaven. Blessed are you when they revile and persecute you, and say all kinds of evil against you falsely for My sake. Rejoice and be exceedingly glad, for great is your reward in heaven, for so they persecuted the prophets who were before you." In 2 Timothy 3:12–13, Paul states, "Yes, and all who desire to live godly in Christ Jesus will suffer persecution. But evil men and impostors will grow worse and worse, deceiving and being deceived." Persecution literally means to "harass, trouble, come against, hurt, or cause distress." This happens on account of our being identified with Christ and teaching His truths. Christ clearly stated to His followers that He was sent into the world to bear witness and His followers will experience persecution. Why? Because the enemy has come to kill, steal and destroy and is incessantly working to prevent the witness and Truth from having its effect of people accepting Christ and responding to the truth. Interestingly, most persecution comes from family members, those we work for and with, fellow believers, and then from those with different religious tenets such as Muslims who wish to eradicate Christianity. This can include governmental regimes such as communists and dictatorships that are just evil and know that Christianity brings thoughts of freedom and fairness, representing a threat to their control. We are not to be surprised by this, and remember that we are not fighting against flesh and blood but against principalities and powers that have direct influence on earth and are against the work of God on earth.

The severity of the persecution ranges from just being ignored and rejected to active pursuit even to the point of imprisonment and death. If we are walking in the Spirit, we all will experience some form of persecution. One of the consequences of living in enemy territory where the enemy is working to oppose us, especially as we are bearing witness to Christ and to His Truth. Most of us only experience modest levels of persecution. This is experienced most often in the form of rejection from family members, fellow workers and bosses, and those with whom

adversity

we have been in friendship. They believe we have fallen for "unhealthy" beliefs and are following a religion that is only an excuse to judge others and think we are "holier than thou." In many cases, this is well deserved and is actually not persecution but adversity caused by our selfishness, as described above. If we move into a "judgment role" and speak judgment against others, we have moved away from walking in the Spirit to the "flesh" and those to whom we speak judgment rightly speak back and react against us. What we think is persecution, is not. It is us causing our own adversity. In most cases, though this rejection is "persecution," as we are just sharing our excitement and joy of living in Christ, and other's anger, fueled by principalities and powers, comes against us, attempting to control us through guilt and rejection. Another form of persecution can be active opposition by those in authority or influence over our careers, business activities, and ministry activities. Due to our stance of faith in Christ, again fueled by principalities and powers, these people react to our righteousness and work to thwart promotions, securing contracts, or set up roadblocks to our progress. The spiritual dynamics of the life of Christ in us bringing truth and light causes those in darkness to hide and push away the light. Since they do not understand these spiritual dynamics, we are the object of their desire to thwart our progress. Another form of persecution is from fellow believers who oppose what we believe and speak because we do not conform to their theology, denominational doctrine, church teaching, etc. This form is the type we have experienced the most. Many fellow believers have actively opposed what we have experienced and taught – that all believers are sheep and can hear the voice of the Shepherd – that He speaks to us personally and that He has an extraordinary plan for our life. Many have openly and publically spoken against us; and they have even worked hard to attempt to convince others that this is wrong theology, and thus, to reject anything taught by us. This persecution endeavors to thwart the work of God through their self-righteous sense of law and judgment – what they believe is the "right way" and their need to convince others that anything else is not to be considered. The more severe forms of persecution range from damaging/destroying belongings, imprisonment and murder. This form is carried out by religious groups like Muslims, government authorities (communist and dictatorships), and rogue sects who believe that eliminating or scaring people away will rid their area of any positive influence that they think stands in the way of their evil control and domination – using force to achieve their objectives – purely demonic, kill, steal and destroy. True persecution comes from the enemy as we are living out Christ in us – is a direct, aggressive attack from Satan attempting to stop the activity of God in a specific location.

Response

As opposed to circumstantial attacks from Satan against which we are to stand and cast off, our response to persecution has different dimensions. Christ states in

adversity

Matthew 5:10–12: that we are "Blessed to be persecuted; that we experience even deeper the kingdom of God; that we are to rejoice and be exceedingly glad; and that we will have a great reward in heaven. Paul states in 2 Timothy 3:10–12 that he endured persecutions and that "out of them all" the Lord delivered him. Stephen and the martyrs of Hebrews 11:36–40 were imprisoned, stoned, slain, and wandered around in desolate conditions. So, first we need to evaluate if our persecution is real or caused by our operating in the flesh. 1 Peter 2:11–12 states that we are to abstain from fleshly lusts which war against the soul (like anger, self-righteousness, attitude of judgment, and selfishness), and conduct ourselves with honor before others. We do this so that when they speak against us as evildoers and twist the truth to make us look bad, they can say nothing about our heart, attitude, or how we presented the truth to them (in love, honor, and respect). This is how we are to glorify God. If we have not been honorable, then it is really not persecution, but adversity caused by our own selfishness. If we have been honorable, then what we are experiencing is persecution. Our response is to first feel blessed, joyful and exceedingly glad – we are on assignment from God; we are living and speaking truth; and we are serving to further God's purpose through inviting others to repent and experience the true Kingdom of God. We then are to ask the Father to strengthen us to endure this, and then provide His instructions to us. He may speak some of the following:

1. *Luke 10:1–12:* **Dust your feet off and leave.** *These people are not interested in receiving your truth and peace, which you have freely*

SECTION 2

and honorably offered; so, no need to spend any more time with them. Do not worry about what they are saying or doing against you. Let it go and move to God's next assignment.

2. *In 2 Timothy 3:10–12,* **God says, "I will deliver you – stay strong, endure, continue to be honorable, respectful and loving, stay speaking truth; Stay here until further instructions. I will either eliminate or make the persecution of no effect (the person or persons going to cease or be removed); or, I will let you know when to leave, and exit this situation. I will call you to another place."** *God has a plan and is only asking you to stay with it a while longer. Resolution is coming. In Daniel 3:1–30, Shadrach, Meshach, and Abed-Nego were faced with either worshiping the golden idol of Nebuchadnezzar or being thrown into the fiery furnace. They believed that God would deliver them but stood on their conviction that no matter the consequences (in this case, death), they would not violate their beliefs. They were thrown into the fire, but were delivered! Christ joined them in the fire and saved them to the extent that their clothes and hair was not even singed, and they did not even smell of smoke. God has the power to deliver us in miraculous ways. Pay attention and be ready to act upon His instruction, including standing on our beliefs and convictions and leaving the outcome to Him.*

adversity

3. *1 Samuel 23:1–13:* **Get out of there now.** *David and his mighty men, when they were being chased down by Saul, had saved the town of Keilah from the attack of the Phillistines. Saul discovered that David was in Keilah and knew that he had David and his men trapped and could kill them all. This an extreme form of persecution. David had defeated Goliath and had been given victory against the Phillistines in battle, and was spared from being found by Saul. He wanted to stay in Keilah, as it was a pleasant place and much more enjoyable than wandering around in caves in the desert. Though it made sense to stay, and he thought that the men of Keilah would protect them since he and his men had saved them, David inquired as to God's instruction. God said to get out of there now, and David did; and Saul stopped his expedition against him for the moment. The key is that we are not to presume we need to stay and accept the persecution, including the dire consequences of the persecution, but rather to seek the Lord who may want us to leave and find a different place where we will not be faced with this persecution.*

4. *Acts 6: 8 – 7: 60:* **God may say to continue to speak the truth, and you will suffer extreme consequences of this life, but He will preserve you through it and bring you your reward in Heaven.** *Stephen was engaged in debate about the truth of God and of Christ. He experienced great power and signs and wonders. He*

spoke the truth openly and was opposed. God did not tell him to dust his feet off, that he would be delivered, or to get out of there. Rather, he was told to stay and continue to speak against this persecution. He gave one of the most eloquent sermons on how Christ fulfills the Old Testament law. The Jewish leaders rejected this truth and took Stephen out to stone him. He was not delivered; but as he was being stoned, Stephen saw heaven open, saw Christ, and knew Christ was taking him home. He was given a special strength to endure the pain for a brief time and had the vision of his eternal destiny that preserved him. Though we have never experienced this personally, we believe that the nature of God gives special preservation and vision through a time such as this. It is not fully understandable other than the Lord fulfills His purposes and glorifies Himself through it. We are not to desire this, but we are also not to be afraid as we will be given special ability to face it and receive our heavenly reward.

So, when we experience persecution (and the Lord says we will, as we bear witness to Him and His life in us), we are to consider ourselves blessed and to rejoice and be exceedingly glad. We are not to just accept this adversity and believe this is our lot in life, but rather to seek the counsel of the Lord. Does he want us to dust our feet off, to experience Him delivering us from it, to leave and get out of there now, or to experience the extreme consequences with special revelation? We are just to ask, and then follow His instruction. The

adversity

type of persecution we have experienced the most is being opposed by fellow believers who do not believe we can hear personally from God. They have spoken against me, written things against me, and worked to have people reject what we have been teaching. First, I feel blessed and rejoice. The Lord asks me to go to forgiveness, and then invite them to explore the truth in the Word together. Few ever were willing to do that. At that point, the Father usually asks me to let it go, dust my feet off, and move on to those who have a heart to hear. In some cases he has delivered me directly from the consequences of the effect that could influence my work or the ministry. A few times he has asked me to get out of there quickly and not receive the planned consequences.

We have never been in a situation where we would experience the dire consequences of property damage, physical harm or death. We are thankful for that, but know that if it ever happened (and in our lifetime, in our country, this is possible), we will be given special ability to endure and then experience our heavenly reward.

chapter 12
HOW DO I KNOW WHICH ADVERSITY I AM FACING?

Usually we know right away – wisdom we have from walking in the Spirit. If we know, we do not second guess, but just proceed according to the wisdom we are receiving as to how the Lord wants to deal with this adversity. Pray through it and respond to God's instructions.

If we are not sure, we can work through the following progression:

1. If we are not regularly abiding in the Vine, in His Word and hearing His Voice, by definition we are walking in the flesh (carnal). Romans 8:5–8 says that when we live in the flesh, we put to death the life of the Spirit in us (as if no effect), are at enmity against God (working against the will of God), and cannot please God

adversity

(not enjoying God's life and purposes in and for us). In essence then, our adversities will be coming from selfishness, which may be leading to discipline, which may be leading to judgment. Probably we are not even considering pruning, though it may be necessary. Certainly, this is not a test of faith, since we are not hearing God speaking promises and truth to us; and this is not likely an attack of Satan either circumstantially or persecution, since we are already putting to death the Spirit, at enmity against God and cannot please God.

2. Is this a test of faith? We will know if we have been receiving Rhema Words from God – promises, prophetic foretelling or forth-telling, truths of transformation, deliverance, etc. As we are abiding in Him, we know what we are being tested on, and thus, are to cooperate with Him in the test and let Him complete our faith and overcome this adversity through this test of faith.

3. Is this pruning? Are we tired, weary, not enjoying our work, our marriage, our family or our ministry? Then something is wrong, and this adversity is meant to get our attention to allow God to cut back our activities, so we can regain margin and sweetness in our life. We are to fully cooperate.

4. Is this general adversity? Has this or is this happening to a wide

group of people or the consequence such as sickness or illness that comes from being in a fallen world? I can sense this is not against me specifically, is not a test of faith or an attack of the enemy – it just is. I am to stay in peace and joy and ask the Father His instruction for how He wishes to resolve this adversity, or how He wishes me to process this adversity.

5. Is this an attack from Satan? I can see that this adversity is coming against me to thwart the will of God and is just wickedness from principalities and powers working either circumstances or persecution against me. I need to stand against the circumstances and ask God to remove this adversity; or I should consider the blessing in the persecution and ask Him to instruct me as how to move forward.

6. If not 2, 3 or 4, then am I experiencing the adversity caused by selfishness. I did not abide in the Vine, did not seek nor follow His will or instructions to me, and I have walked out of His protection and blessing. I need to immediately repent and return to Him and ask Him to resolve this adversity. This is true if the adversity has become more intense leading to discipline or judgment. Repent, return to Him and begin again to abide. Walk with Him and ask Him to bring resolution to what we have

adversity

caused ourselves. He will.

Ask God for wisdom (James 1:5–8) and for clarity and understanding, so you will know how to respond to the adversity. Pray that you do not go to fatalism (whatever happens, happens), nor respond poorly to what is happening.

In almost every situation, regardless of the source, all adversities will move to "a test of faith." The resolution of each involves God's instruction to us regarding what He wants to do to resolve this adversity. Regardless of the source, each one needs resolution. And the resolution requires God to act on our behalf to overcome the adversity. This is something that only He can do, which is always a wonderful opportunity for us to bear witness to the power and wonder of God and for Him to be glorified. Since God said that without faith, it is impossible to please Him and that the just must walk by faith (Hebrews 11:6 and 10:38), in order to resolve our different adversities, He must speak His promises – and then He will ask us to believe with certainty that what He speaks is going to happen (before it happens). As we process this, we will experience the "tests of faith" to reveal our heart and if we do not pass the test, He encourages us to stay with Him for Him to finish our faith. When we had experienced God's judgment (bankruptcy) for my greed, selfishness, and stubbornness of not repenting, our adversity had to be overcome. God

SECTION 2

spoke to us that He would restore our loss. At first, not much happened and we experienced several tests of faith. The question became did we believe what He had spoken to us. We did not pass. We remained in fear and worry; but we stayed abiding and knew that if we continued to walk with God, He would perfect our faith. He did. We came to believe, had peace and joy, and were excited to see how He was going to resolve this adversity. Several miracles happened and our losses were restored.

conclusions

1. **God's original plan was for us to fully enjoy His exceptional life.** He did give mankind free will; and they chose to disobey His instruction and they suffered the consequence. They died. The Holy Spirit departed from their nature and they were now self-centered, sophisticated animals, living in a fallen world characterized by destruction – entropy under the control of the enemy. However, God provided another way of redeeming this condition. Christ was the way, and now we have the chance to again live an exceptional, abundant life in the Sprit. We can live in God's Kingdom of righteousness, peace and joy, while we live in enemy territory where we will experience tribulation and trouble – difficulty, hardship, pain, opposition, frustration, annoyance, etc. We live in two kingdoms, and we are not exempt

from the effects of the fall. As believers, we still have free will, and we can either chose to live in the Kingdom of God through abiding and walking in the Spirit or choose to live carnally, and thus, not experience the benefits of the Kingdom life – just more and more difficulty of the fallen kingdom.

2. **All adversity is not from God or ordained by God**, and thus, we need to understand the causes so that we know how to respond. All the responses are about God, our relationship to God, and what God is doing and will do.

3. **We can avoid completely two sources of adversity, and minimize a third** – Discipline and Judgment (which are from God) never need be experienced if we stay connected to God and repent early in the process when we walk out of the Kingdom due to our self-centeredness. There will be no reason for the Discipline and Judgment, since we are seeking Him and walking with Him. We can minimize the third, which is our causing the adversity due to our self-centeredness and not seeking or listening to God who would have warned us or kept us away from the adversity out there. We can do this by realizing early that we have walked out of the Kingdom and have lost our peace, joy, and freedom. We repent right away and stay in the

adversity

Spirit, thus, minimizing being in the natural adversity caused by ourselves. Regardless of where we are along the path of experiencing adversity due to our own self-centeredness (even if has gone to discipline and judgment), repent now and ask God with His power and sovereignty to overcome this adversity, and redeem the problems caused by ourselves According to Romans 8:28, He can make all things work out for our good, even the problems caused by us. We do need to understand that we still will suffer consequences from discipline and judgment, since we have brought about a path not intended by God. The results of our not walking with God are what they are, and we have to live with them, knowing that God can restore and make it all work. When we went bankrupt, we did lose everything and had to start over. Getting new loans for autos and other things was not easy and was expensive because of my having filed bankruptcy. It prevented us from being able to sell our house right away and purchase another one, so there were consequences. The cool thing is that no matter the mess, we have created (and we have seen some really big ones through our retreat ministry, ones that seem on the surface to be beyond restoration), God redeems and restores, and He can give a new path to an exceptional life. This is truly the Gospel – the Good News!

4. **We all are going to experience general adversity.** Though we live in the Kingdom of God and walking in His protection and power, we are also marching through life in a fallen world that is going to be frustrating and present difficulties. There will be disease, sickness, illness, deformity, disabilities and injuries not related to God-ordained adversity or attacks of Satan. Get over it. It is happening to all those around you, is not directed specifically toward you, and is not from God as a test of faith or an attack from the enemy. Stay in peace; and then ask for wisdom from God regarding how to handle the situation, what is His will, and what He wants us to do. Do not let it grab you and ruin your evening, your weekend, or your week. See it for what it is, and stay in the Kingdom. We can be a wonderful witness to the life of Christ working in us to all involved in this adversity. We should expect this adversity to not continue long or have negative impact against us. One thing we have experienced and understood is that the more willing we are to be pruned back to create margin, space, rest and recreation, the easier it is to deal with general adversity that brings about frustrations. The less we are willing and have crammed our life with stress, over-scheduling, and over-involvements, the more difficult it is to deal with general adversity with its frustrations. The frustrations

adversity

actually contribute to the stress, such that we respond with anger, selfishness, hardness, manipulation, control, and demanding to have our way now. If this is the revelation, the first focus should be on the pruning. It will relieve a lot of the daily stress, and our ability to handle general adversity will be significantly improved.

5. **We will continually experience pruning,** and thus, will have adversities that are intended to show us the need to be pruned and to fully cooperate with God's pruning. This really need not be difficult, yet it is perhaps one of the biggest areas that ultimately cause us to go to selfishness and walk into the natural adversity waiting for us there. This can perhaps lead to discipline and judgment, because we are not responding to God's invitation to pruning. Almost all Americans are too busy, too stressed, and do not know how to relax. This is exacerbated by technology, especially cell phones and emails. We are "on" 24/7, and selfish, demanding people have no problem contacting us and wanting our attention and wanting us to do something for them. So, perhaps it is time to let the Lord prune you back. Start with listing all the things you are involved in throughout a typical week. Get it all down, and let your spouse, kids and friends verify you got it all. Then, get a clean sheet of paper and rebuild what God desires for your life, starting with personal abiding time. If this is not happening,

or you are not willing to put this as top priority, you might as well stop and just realize you are going to have a life of adversity. You will be causing this through self-centeredness. Your abiding time with spouse, family and/or friends (especially if single, you need this); personal enjoyment time with your spouse, family, and/or friends; Sabbath, Holidays and vacations (Linda and I have always, whether we had money or not, have taken at least a weekend off and spent time together at a place away from our home); then your occupation – the work or place of interest where you spend most of your weekday time; then one ministry activity of "giving it away" where you see God at work and is an activity that brings out your passion and gifts. Basically, everything else on your list needs to cease. Work at living out your life with these priorities and see if you start to experience "sweetness" about all aspects of your life. Keep working at it until you have pruned back to this sweetness. Once there, then at least once a quarter, review what has crept in and readjust back to the sweetness. There we will truly experience the best of God's abundant life for us, and we will see big time fruit. In the transformation of our nature, in the supernatural work of God, and the joy of seeing others come alive in Christ and get connected to the vine and walk with God. Most everyone we share this with says, "Yeah, but these organizations and activities all require my involvement. If I stop, they will fall apart." What a croc! All it means is that you are playing God and have determined that being a Martha is better than being a Mary, although Christ said that Mary was the one who had chosen best. Why would you not be allowed to be pruned until you are in a position to live a truly sweet life and bear fruit, more fruit, and even more fruit?

6. **If this adversity is a test of faith by God, then fully cooperate.** We will and should be experiencing these tests all the time, since without faith it is impossible to please Him. We should have no trouble identifying if this is a test of faith, as faith is authored by God speaking a promise or truth to us personally (Rhema). If we have already heard this, then we understand that He has declared a promise to us; and we are processing this with our spouse or friend. We are conscious of it, speaking of it, and spending abiding time with the Father on it. Thus, we would know that the adversity being experienced is directly about testing, whether we believe this promise or not. If we are not hearing God or His promises, the scripture says our hearts have been drawn away. Interestingly, many have always lived without hearing from God, because they have been taught it's not possible and that hearing from God is heresy. This is so sad. If we have no promises being spoken to us,

it means the adversity we are facing is due to one of the other causes above.

If it is a test of faith and we know it, then instead of asking God to remove it and being upset about it, ask God to reveal to you why you are having difficulty believing, and ask Him to transform the wound or destructive pattern in you that He desires to heal. As we gain understanding of our reaction to general adversity, both of these will reveal our growth in the fruit of the Spirit, which is our nature being transformed into the nature of Christ. This is where it is no longer I that live but Christ in me. We cannot produce our own fruit, so our call is not to work at it or try harder. This actually makes it worse, so we are to just abide in Him and He will do the transforming work. We and those around us will notice it.

Spend time journaling your heart and your response to what God is speaking to you from His Word. Ask for revelation and wisdom, in order to know what is in the way of true faith. Stay abiding, dialoguing, praying, and sharing with others until He finishes it. You have certainty that the adversity that is the test does not affect you. You know that you know that you know, and you have the confidence that it will be performed as the Father has spoken.

You pass the test! And you will see the adversity go away and the promise fulfilled, though always in His timing, which is usually longer than ours.

7. **We will be attacked specifically by the enemy, either through circumstances or persecution.** Remember 1Peter 5:8 says, "Be sober, be vigilant; because your adversary the devil walks about like a roaring lion, seeking whom he may devour." The enemy is real and is prowling constantly as an adversary against Christians, seeking to make use of every opportunity to destroy us (cause us to experience circumstances that ruin our lives, our relationships, our life with God and lead us to broken heartedness, discouragement, despair, and resignation).

We need to fully comprehend that we are targets of the enemy who is pursing us. Thus, that the adversities and difficulties being brought on by the enemy are not just natural things, but rather, they are being driven by principalities and powers that are operating behind the scenes. When we are operating outside of God's Kingdom, we are no match for principalities and powers. However, inside of God's Kingdom, the demonic powers have zero ability to influence and attack us. So, the enemy's strategy is to tempt us or draw us out of the Kingdom through our own self-centeredness, and then to keep us out of the Kingdom, particularly by not abiding in or seeking to walk with God. Through their observation, these demonic powers can see our patterns, and thus, the arrows are thrown more frequently so that we fall back into that pattern. The enemy is constantly scheming to develop strategies that bring adversity against us and cause us to fall. He usually uses other people who are captive to His influences through anger, bitterness, hardness, extreme self-centeredness, controlling, manipulating, and other perverse conditions of their hearts. They do things that come against us in our business, marriage, family, children, ministry, community, etc. They serve as roadblocks to our work, success, and enjoyment by causing negative circumstances and failure to come against us. The principalities and powers, having seen ways that draw us out of the Kingdom and prevent us from walking with God, stimulate the circumstances that are directly coming against us. Mostly, Satan uses selfish people who have power and authority to cause trouble and difficulty in our circumstances. The enemy is using these selfish, manipulating, controlling people to thwart God's will for us, cause trouble, create obstacles, etc. What we thought was on track all of a sudden falls off the rails, because the enemy is attacking us through this circumstance. His goal is

adversity

to destroy our plan and to destroy our heart, so we will fall into discouragement, fear, and worry.

Knowing that we are fighting against principalities and powers, it is critical to understand that we can only fight against these in the spirit and with God's weapons and not our natural abilities. We fight with:

- **The belt of truth**

- **The breastplate of righteousness**

- **The gospel of peace on our feet**

- **The shield of faith**

Up to this point, all of the weapons have been defensive and only operate if we are facing the battle. We are using them to protect and to quench anything that the enemy can throw at us. At this point we then turn to the offense and go after the enemy directly.

- **The sword of the word:** We now use the very promise and the truths of God to go against the enemy and to bind him and cast him out of the situation. Jesus gave us binding and loosing, as the keys to the Kingdom. We stand on the truth and speak the truth, and this causes the enemy to flee and not be able to accomplish His goal of thwarting God's will. We then return to

God's beautiful fulfillment of our circumstances, without the pressure and adversity from the enemy.

- **Prayer:** Throughout the process we constantly stay in prayer – in fellowship with God – as we walk with Him utilizing these weapons and accomplishing the ability to stand and withstand the attack of the enemy.

If it is from persecution, we are to consider ourselves blessed, and rejoice and be exceedingly glad. Then, we are to ask the Father how He wishes to resolve this adversity and our course of action regarding this adversity:

- **Dust our feet off**

- **Wait for God to deliver us**

- **Get out of there now**

- **Stay and suffer the consequences (even the dire ones), knowing that we will be given special strength to endure and have a vision of our Heavenly reward**

So, if you consider all these, our first and best place to be is walking in the Spirit, letting Him guide and lead us into His promised abundant life. (Seek ye first the Kingdom of God and His righteousness, and ALL these things will be added to you). General adversity will not trap

adversity

us, and we will be able to live a joyful life in the middle of a world of frustration and trouble that befalls us all. We also will fully cooperate with His pruning process, and realize how critical and how wonderful is the pruning in moving us and keeping us in a life of sweetness. Thus, we will avoid any adversity from discipline and judgment and minimize our adversities caused by self-centeredness, since the longer we abide and walk in the Spirit, our sensitivity to our selfishness will be acute; and when we lose our peace, joy and freedom, we will recognize it and return back to the relationship. In doing this, we avoid the adversities that might come, because we are not being directed by the Father away from them. Then, we will be able to discern between the attacks of the enemy and tests of faith from God. If the adversity is from the enemy, we stand against it and chase it away through the spiritual weapons available to us, knowing that when we are in Christ he has to flee, as he has been defeated. If it's from God, we fully cooperate, let Him process us through to greater faith, serving His purposes. Our adversities will be understood fully, and none will cause us to lose our peace, joy and freedom. Life truly will be exceptional!

SECTION 2

More resources by Richard T. Case:

Available wherever fine books are sold!

elevate publishing

A strategic publisher empowering authors to strengthen their brand.

Visit Elevate Publishing for our latest offerings.
www.elevatepub.com

www.ingramcontent.com/pod-product-compliance
Lightning Source LLC
Chambersburg PA
CBHW071741080526
44588CB00013B/2112